SUNRISE AT SUNSET

SUNRISE AT SUNSET

*My Story of Transformation
after a Hemorrhagic Stroke*

Steve Wewerka

ISBN: 979-8-9908100-0-6 paperback
ISBN: 979-8-9908100-1-3 ebook
ISBN: 979-8-9908100-2-0 audio

See www.stevewewerka.com to learn more about the author.

Cover design by Steve Wewerka
Photographs by Steve Wewerka
Edited by Amy Phillips
Book design by Rudy Ramos

*To Andy and Lucas,
my sons and my foundation,
who kept me going through
my worst moments.*

TABLE OF CONTENTS

— ACKNOWLEDGMENTS —

Throughout the year-and-a-half that it took to write *Sunrise at Sunset*, many, many people helped me. They are too numerous to mention here, but I owe them a debt of gratitude. The wonderful professionals who helped me recover and rehabilitate at Advocate Lutheran General Hospital and Shirley Ryan Ability Lab Physical Therapy must be recognized. Without them, I don't know where I would be. My friend Sandy graciously made space for me in her home when I needed a place to live during the early stages of my recovery. Without her friendship and support, my healing would have been vastly diminished. Lastly, I'd like to thank my editor, Amy Phillips, who helped me to polish a message I hope readers will find helpful and meaningful.

— PREFACE —

What would you do if your life were stripped away in a few heartbeats? Take a minute to think about this. What's the worst thing to ever happen to you? How did you find your way out of that place? In that journey are the roots to your survival.

Suffering a hemorrhagic stroke sucks! You're cruising along the road of life, comfortable in your lane and in an instant….

Nothing prepares you for a traumatic physical event. Nothing. All your carefully made life plans are gone. Goals, dreams, and desires simply evaporate as your priorities shift from a future of possibilities to survival. The first few days are a desperate time. As you sink into hopelessness, you are filled with fear and are physically vulnerable.

After my stroke, I needed help with almost every aspect of my life. Being rolled out of bed into a wheelchair made a simple restroom visit a twenty-minute exercise in bladder control. The questions pile up, and answers are hard to find. The emotional shock of a life-altering traumatic experience ripped deep into my assumptions of life. Why me? How will I survive? Does my life still have value?

I am one of the lucky ones. I made it through the first day. Only one out of five hemorrhagic stroke victims survives that first twenty-four hours. Fortunately, I was visiting friends in Chicago who found me immediate help, and I was a seven-minute ambulance ride from a major neural center. Most importantly, my bleed was in an area of my brain that didn't kill me instantly.

The reason I had a stroke might have been fate or divine intervention or simply the roll of the dice. Determining which of those held sway is beyond my ability to fathom. I do know this: I am very fortunate. As bad as this was, it could have been much worse.

At first, instead of choosing acceptance, I got in my own way. I fought. I battled to hold on to the past. I wanted to prove to everybody that I was smart. I, on my own, could beat this because I had always been self-reliant. I knew I could depend on myself. I wouldn't let myself down. It is hard to let go of decades of survival skills. My coping technique has always been about controlling my personal narrative and keeping everyone at a distance. I never accepted help because I feared I would be judged and belittled. I thought everyone would make fun of me or see me as a fraud or failure. "Help" was a four-letter word in my self-assigned isolation.

Day after day, layer by layer, I was stripped of what I thought was my dignity. I came to understand it wasn't dignity but pride. That pride was built from years of living a life defined by unrealistic, unhealthy expectations of what I thought I should be. Eventually I gave in to the fact that there was nothing the old me could do. I let go. I released the aura of expectations. "This is where I am, and this has happened to me," I told myself. Hemorrhage. Stroke. Left arm and leg, paralyzed.

This was a pivotal moment: I could cling to my past, believing that something was stolen from me and letting my stroke define me as a victim, or I could change my attitude and continue to energetically live my life. At first, I settled into a neutral acceptance, and I eventually gained a profound understanding of self-awareness.

I found comfort in taking on the challenge of recovery. I focused on the goal of getting my life back. I accepted and anticipated the opportunity to discover a new sense of self. I saw my hemorrhagic stroke as a means of self-reflection and as a catalyst for positive change.

Every morning, I chose an optimistic internal dialogue: "Let go of the past, and accept what is to unfold." Through this simple mantra, I found the resolve to keep living, to do the work necessary to heal and discover what I could achieve.

I realized the hemorrhagic stroke couldn't be my focus for recovery. That was just something that happened to me. It was a major, life-changing event. So was having children or moving to a new city. Instead, I had to choose how I wanted to live and how to play the game of life, no matter what cards I was dealt.

I am fortunate that my fundamental approach to work and life are based on the idea of adaptation and flexibility. I make my living as a landscape photographer. The success of my work depends on the acceptance of chance. The difference between a brilliant image and a mundane photo is bound to the weather. If I scout photo opportunities with a rigid idea in mind and am not open to chance, I will miss seeing what Mother Nature has to offer. This perspective has given me not only the tools to continue my artistic aspirations but also the courage to face the challenges of a potentially diminished life. Adapt and pivot. Without flexibility, preconceived ideas lock us on a fixed point.

My creativity reaches into every aspect of my life, not just photography. It's not the "craft"—or the technical expertise of creating—that makes me an artist; it's my desire to express my experiences and insights, to tell my story. That's a story of living in the twenty-first century. When I looked at my dramatic life change from a healthy perspective, I realized I had just been handed a gift, a new way of understanding the world. I could use my decades of creative experience to further share my journey.

I began to share my recovery experiences with readers on my social media sites. I found an eager community of support there. My story touched more people than I could have imagined, many with their own traumatic experiences. They also shared my journey with loved ones who found solace in my words. My self-esteem and confidence found a footing as my creativity emerged through my writing. Each day I documented my experiences, providing me with a positive personal achievement that carried into my recovery attitude. I set a small goal and reached it every day. Writing these vignettes gave me a sense of purpose and, most importantly, daily victories.

For months I revealed glimpses into my journey, writing them in the moment as I found the words to convey an honest expression of my feelings. I wrote about the raw, emotional experiences and my progress as I regained control over my body. As I rediscovered the fundamental, almost primal joy of walking, I explored thoughts about myself as I reexamined my values. For the first time, I critically reflected on how I had been living my life. For example, I inflated minor, everyday irritants into unnecessary, seemingly life-influencing events. I made assumptions with no attempt to seek clarification. I let resentments build and become justifications for isolating myself. At the same time, I obsessed about trying to fit in. I realized that with my attention fixated on the easy answers, I didn't have to explore the complex nature of my personality. I didn't have to question why I pulled away from everyone. In my heart, I knew I was living in a self-destructive cycle. I was running away from myself and any chance I had of maintaining healthy relationships with others.

As I wrote, I discovered my attitude had set me up for an empty, unfulfilled, and frustrating life. My stroke taught me to ask questions and seek explanations when I am unsure of the message. Most importantly, I now know I am doing the best I can in the moment. I don't have to be perfect. I can learn and do better in the future.

Writing each day helped me to explore my ever-evolving spiritual awareness, and I worked to infuse an optimistic perspective into my words. Losing myself—my old self—was a cleansing process that created room to rework my life into a vision of who I wanted to become. I took time to reflect and find answers to questions I previously did not know to ask. Removing myself from my regular interactions and influences stripped away the unnecessary chatter. Slowly and organically, my self-perception changed. Not only do I now see myself clearly, but I also have a better understanding of my life and how I want to live it.

My life is not a passive journey. I am an active participant. I choose to tackle the obstacles tossed onto my path. I am a stroke survivor standing at a crossroads. I didn't lose my life; I was gifted an appreciation for the value of every breath. My trauma is a chance to live, something few people experience after such an event. Because I seek enlightenment through experiencing life, I choose to see it as an opportunity to expand my knowledge and self-awareness and to grow into a better man.

My choice is simple: spend life as a victim or get busy living it. Every day I make choices that affect my actions. Some are profound moments of inspired insight. Others are less conscious but still lead to subtle progress.

I don't live my life in fear because fear traps the mind in the past. It draws on my most powerful memories, which influence how I interpret the present. My personal history and experiences provide the blueprint of how to navigate my life, but without a measure of reflection, they can freeze me in place when it is crucial to be open to change. Life is not a problem to be solved; it is an opportunity for experience.

As the days turned to weeks and then months, I learned to accept my new normal. The "what I was" was replaced with "who I am." The hemorrhage in my brain will always be a piece of me. It has inherently altered my life and will continue to do so. Six months after my stroke, I still had daily struggles. My energy was limited. Most days I rested throughout the day. I continue to improve. I've embraced the experience of recovery. I cherish all my tiny successes and try to accept the process.

This book is divided into two major sections. The majority of text describes my rehabilitation, both in and out of the hospital, as daily entries. The first three installments I wrote from memory. I added them to give continuity to the timeline. The rest are voiced each day as I lived them. Reading back through my daily musings, I found that most needed additional explanation or analysis because I discovered a deeper appreciation for my experiences as I have continued to heal. These additions follow each entry and are in italics. The second part of the book contains short essays on insights and strategies I've taken to heart so that I can live the life I choose. There is hope after a traumatic physical event, and perhaps sharing my experiences can help others who might be going through similar challenges to find peace, happiness, and personal growth.

—STEVE WEWERKA

June 2024

PART I: **REHAB DAYS**

— CHICAGO —

My first thoughts after my stroke came in flashes:

This is really bad, and a pill ain't gonna fix this mess.
My world as I know it … is … well … gone.
I don't know how to do this.

With every breath, I'd find a new reason that my life sucked. No one had answers. I was angry. I was desperate. I was sad. I was fearful that each breath might be my last.

I didn't know how to comprehend what was happening because in all my years of life, I had never experienced anything that came close to the emotional and physical trauma of becoming paralyzed within a few heartbeats. I had suffered a hemorrhagic stroke. I could have died, but I survived and had to face the unknowns of recovery.

Tests and more tests.

The nurses woke me up to see if I was still alive and then told me I needed my rest. I was afraid to go to sleep because I kept wondering, *What if I don't wake up?*

I didn't know what to feel or how to feel. I was vulnerable. I needed help with everything. I have never felt so helpless, so small and pitiful and inadequate. I couldn't go to the bathroom by myself. I needed two people to move me from my bed. I hated the call button. I associated it with failure. The more I pushed that button, the more my dignity dimmed.

The first step in the healing process is acceptance. You must make peace with where you are, not how or why you ended up there. Simply accept your situation.

Day 1: Saturday, December 17, 2022

I had just won five hundred bucks! That was the last thing that happened before a capillary in the center of my head burst, and blood flooded into my brain.

The Windy City was living up to its winter reputation. A friend and I arrived early for our dinner reservation near downtown Chicago, and instead of standing around in the cold, we decided to wait at a nearby casino. We watched football and had a drink. Then I sat at a blackjack table. I honestly don't remember what I was feeling. Maybe I was a bit off; I'm not sure. My memories immediately before the "event" are of just random, daily occurrences.

The cheapest table was $25. I was doing well, adding to my winnings. Within a few hands, I had made $125 on my cards. I got a split and two double downs for a total of $500 riding on chance. The dealer went bust. He lost, and I won.

As I stared at the stack of twenty green chips in front of me, I felt (or saw, I'm not sure which) a sense of light gusting through my head. Visually, it was like windblown snow caught in the light of a streetlamp, diminishing in the distance and creating the feeling of being in a tunnel. No headache. No dizziness. I just felt a bit off. The feeling did not dissipate, and I said to my friend, "I need to get some fresh air." I tried to stand and could not.

Within twenty minutes, I was receiving a CAT scan, and my life changed forever.

I never lost consciousness. I was doling out one-liners with the paramedics on the way to the ER. When I get nervous, I tend to talk. That's how I tried to control the narrative so no one could tell me what I don't want to hear. I thought, "This is just a pinched nerve or something insignificant." At that time, I could not have imagined what was coming.

Day 2: Sunday, December 18, 2022

I'm not sleeping much. Every hour a nurse checks in on me. I'm hooked to many devices. Noise. There's lots of mechanical noise. Every sound reminds me that I am totally lost and at the mercy of the beeping, hissing wall of machines.

I feel so alone. I don't want anyone to see me as this broken, vulnerable, papier-mâché shell of myself. I'm sinking deeper into a self-imposed, emotional exile. Who do I tell? How can I control this narrative? Who can I trust? I can't ask anyone to carry my burden, emotional or physical. I've lost control.

I'll find footing where I can. I can still use my right hand. Except for the shock of having a stroke, my mind and thoughts seem to be mostly intact. Stroke? Let's not call it that. That's what strikes down old people. Cerebral hemorrhage. The doctors and nurses call it a hemorrhagic stroke. Blood has leaked into my brain and has messed me up.

At this point, I thought the stroke was a small thing. I was confident that in a few days, I'd be back on my feet, living my life as I always had, my plans intact and my goals still on the horizon for me to meet.

Day 3: Monday, December 19, 2022

I cannot understand what happened. The doctors don't have any answers. "Just wait and see" isn't comforting. I need answers. I crave something, *anything*, to hold on to. I'm not the kind of person who can let go of control. I need to anticipate my next move. Without knowing the rules, how can I play the game? I feel as if I am floating on an invisible swirling current, spinning from hopeful to sad to hopeful to sad.

I let myself feel the raw emotions of loss and cling to any hope

I can muster. Instead of burying my emotions, I am living them as they come crashing in and then subside. I cry in my private moments. I cry a lot. It feels healthy to release.

I am not … what I was. But I am still me. My body is broken, yet I think and feel the same in my head. My mind is intact. This is what I will cling to in dark moments. I have an inner strength and the ability to believe in who I am. I trust in my general disposition that every day is an opportunity to be more than I was the day before.

My stroke is horribly hard and sad. It's life altering in ways I cannot fathom yet. My resilience and my desire to live life through new experiences will help me move forward. I can see my life through a new set of eyes.

Looking back at this moment, I realize I was flying my emotional box kite in a hurricane. No matter how I held the string, it was burning my hands as it flew deeper into the storm. I was scrambling to find anything to hold my mind steady. I felt so alone. I didn't want to ask for help, and I was embarrassed by how weak I had become—physically and emotionally. I cried a lot. Uncontrollable tears poured down my cheeks. I sobbed out loud. And somehow, in the middle of setting my emotions free, I felt the beginnings of a way forward. I found the first steps to acceptance. No one judged me. They just let me be, let me work though my trauma. This was the best thing for me because I was able to vent or evacuate this new overwhelming set of crazy emotions. I didn't try to hold them inside, and that gave me room to see myself again. I eventually circled back to my core values. I realized I had a good sense of self, and I just needed to approach this problem from a new angle. I wrote to my friends and community of artists and asked for help. The following entry is that request.

Day 4: Tuesday, December 20, 2022

I'm going to ask you to take a journey with me.

Saturday night a blood vessel in my brain burst. The doctors don't know why. I have no underlying medical issues.

I'm told I nearly died. The pressure on my brain shocked my muscular system, and I've lost control of my left arm and left leg. I can't walk. Everything I do requires help. It seems my tear ducts are the only things working normally. The doctors are confident that with intensive rehab, I will walk again in a few months. Maybe drive in six months. Art fairs, the way I make my living and share my life's work, well, that's a question for the future. That means I have to fundamentally change the way I live my life and, more importantly, how I continue to share my work.

I live with intention; I truly want to make the world a better place filled with peace and contentment. This gives my life purpose and aligns with my personal values. I am challenged right now. I'm trying to make sense of it all. Every moment is a battle. I hate relying on or asking anyone for help. Yet as I lie here, body broken,

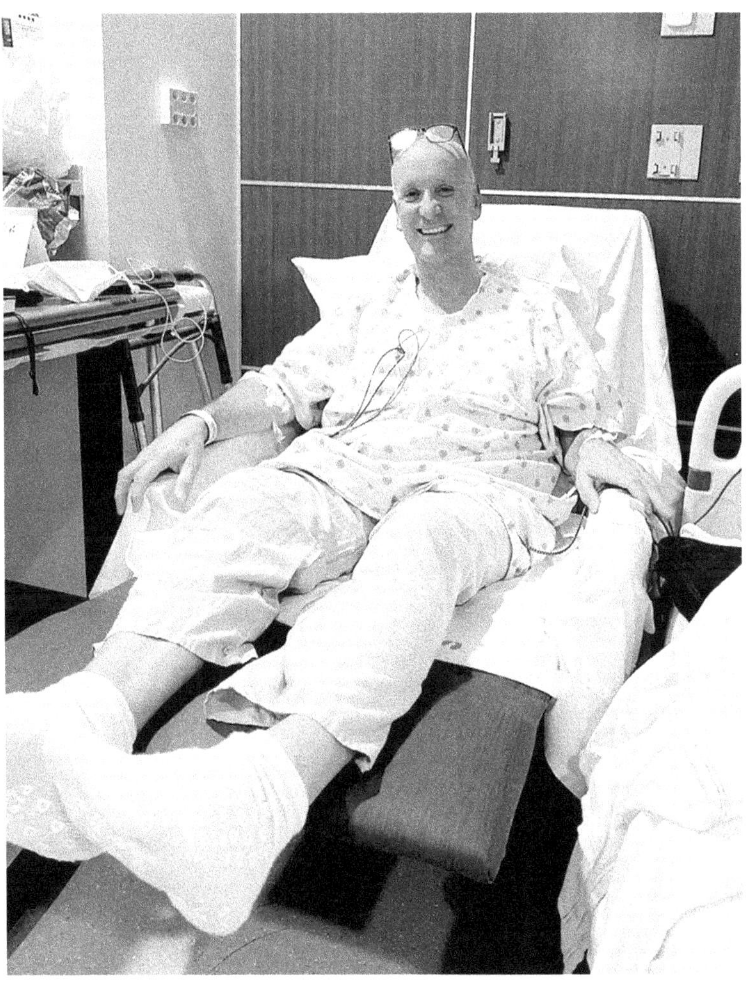

During the first days in my hospital room, I needed help with every task. My life was tied to a call button.

my mind is racing like a driver on the autobahn. I have to find a different approach to my work.

I normally sell my images at art fairs across the country, driving place to place in my Sprinter van and capturing moments in time as I go. But now I can't, and I need to find a different way to reach people. Let's do this together, a little differently than before. Go to my website, www.stevewewerka.com, and find a new piece of art for your life. Find something that speaks to you. Purchasing a piece will absolutely help with bills, but more importantly, it supports my desire to share the unique way I see the world. You will be reaffirming that I am making a difference, that I am *more*, that my life's work has purpose, that I've touched your life.

It's funny how new, unplanned chapters unfold right as things seem to be coming into place. I've worked hard to find my way, and I've just started to tell my story. I have much more to tell, and with your help, I can.

Thank you so much.

Steve

I always have alternatives. Recognizing that is one of my survival skills. The Boy Scout in me is always ready for life to go wrong. As I struggled to find something to keep my world from spinning into the black void of my emotional version of space, I cut the seal on that jar of well-preserved emergency plans. In truth, none of my plans could work in this situation. That prompted me to address two questions: 1) What was my biggest concern? and 2) What was impeding me from accepting my life as forever changed? I had charted a path and suddenly found myself on a new journey. I realized it was about being self-reliant. It hit me that I needed to pivot and look at financial and creative goals from the perspective of this new path. I was not out of the game; I simply needed to change how I played it. I decided to start sharing my story to fulfill my creative needs. I asked friends, colleagues, and clients to continue purchasing my work but to do it through my online store instead of coming to me directly.

Day 5: Wednesday, December 21, 2022

You are familiar with my current situation. And I really don't want to leap into the self-pity pit, although I stand at its edge about every fifth heartbeat.

I'm adapting to new routines. Before this event, most mornings I meditated while I walked. It's how I greeted the day. The rhythm of walking cleared my mind as I set aside the distractions of daily life. Eventually I would find my authentic voice whispering to me. It took me months to recognize the difference. Most of my thoughts, to a large degree, were influenced by the external noise of other people's opinions. With careful listening, I could distinguish my voice from the external ones. I would write "my" thoughts.

Right now, walking is not an option. I guess I could kind of roll. Ha! Picture that, a fifty-seven-year-old rolling like a log down a hill! Not a majestic sight. The physical will come in time. The crucial part of my routine is to continue having honest internal conversations. The process of writing forces me to organize my thoughts. I can find a rhythm similar to walking. I focus on what I am feeling and what I want to write.

Telling stories is how we relate to each other, how we find and build a common connection, and how we nurture our community.

(Taking a break. My head hurts.)

Sorry, I'm spent. Here's my thought for the day: If you spend your time thinking about where you want to be instead of how to get there, you will never be anywhere.

These daily musing became my lifeline. Being stuck in a hospital bed and depending on help for most my daily needs could have resulted in slipping into a bleak emotional pit of despair. Writing every day gave me purpose. Without an outlet for my creative energy, I would have lost my sense of self. Being an artistic person, I need to express my insights and ideas. I would write my thoughts throughout the day. Eventually a patten would surface. Most days I never knew what I was going to share until the next morning. The process of organizing my ideas created a routine that motivated me. I looked forward to every day as a new experience to share. It gave me a sense of control at a time when I depended on so many others for help.

Day 6: Thursday, December 22, 2022

I'm having a hard time emptying my mind and getting focused. The reason is that I begin intensive rehab today. I am very anxious about it. The next part of my life rotates around what happens with my body over the next two weeks. I will get a true assessment of the extent of its physical damage and a rough timeline for recovery. Even though I am worried, my routine gives me a stable vantage point to face my challenges. I see my routine as something I have control over. I must bow to the unknown and the process, trusting the professionals to guide me down my recovery path. It's not necessarily giving in or giving up. It's accepting that change is the only constant.

I had so many questions. The stack of unknowns was scary. This was the first step toward living an independent life.

Day 7: Friday, December 23, 2022

When I was in my early twenties, I had a summer job guiding whitewater raft trips in southern Colorado. I knew a guy back then who would find any reason to get drunk. One night he threw a party because his male puppy had lifted its leg to pee. I guess it was a party celebrating the transformation from puppy to adult male "dog-hood."

One small bit of freedom in my life is that now I can, with assistance, use a walker to move around a little bit. physical therapy yesterday was literally the first step toward freedom. The person assisting me into the bathroom put the toilet seat down. I said, "No, leave it up." Woof, woof.

Today, let's celebrate the small victories and tiny transformations.

Happy holidays everyone. Knowing you're out there and with me on my journey means more to me than you can imagine.

The quality of my rehab experience was due to both the amazing staff at the hospital and my desire to walk again. I was fragile. My left leg and arm did not respond to my intuitive commands. With focused thought and attention, I could get a halting, unsteady response. Not enough to confidently move, but at this point any movement was an improvement. Day one of rehab was mostly about finding a baseline of how severely debilitated I was. With the staff's help and confidence, I took my first steps using a walker.

Day 8: Saturday, December 24, 2022

I woke in the middle the night thinking about miracles—not so much the God-driven kind, but the amazing people who have taken root in my life. An incredible number of people have sent me notes, said prayers on my behalf, and shared with me how my life's work has touched them. An overwhelming number have bought work from me. I am truly blown away by the outpouring of support. I've had the opportunity to experience something few people get to. Mostly, it's our family members that hear about how wonderful we are—after we die. I cannot, in any way whatsoever, communicate adequately the amount of joy I feel. I am blessed, and *you*, friends, are my Christmas miracle. Thank you. Merry Christmas and happy holidays. I love you all. (Now if I could only find those two front teeth.)

I learned about true unconditional graciousness and gratitude in that first week. I wrongly had assumed that the good qualities of humanity had been stripped away by the rigors of modern life. Hundreds of friends and colleagues reached out to express care and concern. People sent me notes and bought prints from my website. Having that financial support removed one of the most stressful aspects of my life. I am so thankful. Without their support, my outcome may have been much more tenuous.

Day 9: Sunday, December 25, 2022

Nights are the hardest. I wake up, and as I stare into the darkness, my optimism wavers. Negative thoughts of never being independent or having another stroke force their way onto my consciousness.

I have no one to turn to for help. My pride won't let me call for a nurse. I don't want them to know how much I struggle at night. I am afraid they will overreact and take away the tiny amount of self-determination I possess. Just today I convinced them I don't need the bed alarm that alerts the caregivers when someone tries to get out of bed. I talk myself back to sleep. I remind myself that life is full of uncertainties.

Life's about making choices. How do I want to live in the future? How I live today affects the outcome tomorrow, so I'm shaping my future life today. I do that through my actions, thoughts, and behaviors. I'm making a positive emotional investment today because I want to have a positive tomorrow. I can't worry about the future. All I can do is work and create opportunities for the future to unfold in a way that gives me choices.

I'm going to be me in the future, and if I don't like who I am today, then I'm not going to like my future self. It's a matter of adjusting who I am now so that in the future I turn out to be the person I want to be.

When everything you know is stripped away, all that is left is the raw you. I spent a lot of time fighting the voices in my head that wanted to drag me down. I had to evaluate my life and come to terms with a few unpleasant aspects of myself. I had shaped my physical world to distance myself from others, and I lost myself along the way. I had built a fortress that reinforced an illusion of my world. Instead of challenging myself to understand why I had been hurt and owning my role in that pain, I justified my walls by blaming those who I thought had injured me. Having to rely on the kindness of everyone was a chance to reset my outlook, to really dig into my hard-set beliefs to find trust in myself and to drop my misguided mistrust of humanity.

Day 10: Monday, December 26, 2022

I've had a lot of rough moments. As much as I try to set my intentions—being positive, work hard, understand the process, and be realistic—*this* still beats me up: I realize I have been focusing on an arbitrary point in time that has become crystallized in my mind as the measure of success or failure. Why am I not getting there faster? I want to be me again.

It is important to have goals in rehab, not an outcome that becomes an anchor to which I attached a mountain of expectations. The goals are simple: work the process, let the journey unfold as my body heals, and toss out the timeline.

Staying in the present is important. I must acknowledge my feelings in the moment. I'm up, I'm down, I'm sad, I'm happy. It's part of the process of understanding who I am now. It all comes down to acceptance.

Committing to this path I am forced to travel means realizing I have little control. I have no knowledge of what is to come and no framework from past experiences to fall back on. It is all new and uncharted. Thinking about unrealistic possibilities blinds me to the work ahead and the positive progress I have made. Acceptance means keeping my head in the present.

It is a scary headspace, not having control. I rely on taking tiny steps, testing my footing as I go. I'm creating emotional stability as well as physical grounding. Fixating on the summit of the mountain while ignoring where I place my feet will not get me to the top safely.

Every day I was finding new meaning in my recovery. I think we all know that appreciating the tiny steps in life's journey is much more important than reaching the destination, but embracing that as a personal philosophical mantra was new to me.

Day 11: Tuesday, December 27, 2022

I don't know where this day went. Physical therapy is beating me up. My body is tired. I don't feel pain as much as weariness. The physical exertion without the reward of success weighs heavy on my mind. I'm not improving fast enough. I feel trapped, and my lack of progress consumes my thoughts. Everything takes so much longer to accomplish. Fulfilling my bathroom needs, although only a seven-step journey, takes a phone call to the nurse for assistance. Then I must maneuver my way out of bed into safe shoes, be helped up to the walker, and then unsteadily shuffle to the loo, grab a safety railing, and somehow keep my dignity while someone watches over me.

It feels like being in the ocean and riding the cycles of the current. There are moments when I am at the top of the crest, full of optimism, and others when I am in the trough, blinded to all but what is right in front of me.

These were the normal cycles of recovery. The rehab staff wanted me to push my body. Delaying would have made it harder for my brain and muscles to reconnect. They needed me to do the work if I wanted to recover. A speedy recovery was not the issue; the repetition of movement would reconnect and retrain my brain and body. Looking back at this day and how I was feeling, I can see I was mourning how much I had lost. The amount of energy I needed for physical therapy was a fraction of what I needed to live a normal day. In retrospect, I should have given myself a mental hug and been proud of the progress I had made in just a few days.

Day 12: Wednesday, December 28, 2022

My morning rituals are very important to me. One reason I write every morning is the sense of accomplishment. Even before I start the hard work, I have accomplished a personal, self-nurturing goal. I set the tone for my day. Figurative steps into a positive headspace.

After my vitals are taken each morning, I ask the nurse to bring me a cup of ice. I like to drink a small can of cola. My goal is to pour it using my left hand. Today was the first day I felt confident enough to go for it. After moving everything out of the way on the hospital table, I aligned the mouth of the can over the cup. I had good control of my fine motor skills. I was able to hold a can without a lot of shaking.

I greet each day by watching the sunrise. (It was spectacular today.) Because there are so many mechanical noises in this room, I keep the lights off. It feels more natural to watch the sun rise in the dark. I had the can in my left hand. I was ready. I felt steady. And as I began to pour ... the soda flowed all over the table. I laughed out loud. Even though I had set a perfect intention, had a solid goal in mind, and had a plan for a successful pour, I couldn't see that the lid was still on my cup.

Today is going to be an amazing. I'm still able to laugh at my silly stuff.

In my previous post, I was struggling with my body and emotional issues. In this one, I celebrated small goals and made fun of myself. This is the nature of recovery. It is a day-to-day and even an hour-to-hour process. I intellectually knew what I was capable of physically achieving; I have a lifetime of memories to draw from. Yet I was like a toddler learning to walk. This is another example of needing to accept the process and to focus on the moment.

Day 13: Thursday, December 29, 2022

Yesterday I had a long talk with my primary physical therapist. Was I getting in the way of my recovery? Was I too focused on an outcome?

He said, "Your body is broken. If you don't slow down and think about each part of a movement and step with intention, your brain won't learn how to do it properly."

This made me think about the difference between emotional and physical intentions. My physical needs right now are distorted by my drive for outcomes: to walk, drive, photograph, and so on, so that I can return to my independent life.

My goal is to continue living my life in the best possible way in alignment with my personal values, the principles that guide my sense of right and wrong. I follow what makes me content, joyful, and at peace. When faced with a hard decision, I can make a choice based on my values. The right choice is not always the easiest one, but I can act without fear because of my values.

My physical challenges cloud my intentions. Let me try to explain. My primary value is to be of service to others and ask nothing in return. This brings me more joy than just about anything else. My photography is not about me. I share my images to capture the beauty of life, and I hope they brighten the viewer's day. Needing so much help runs contrary to my nature. I am pushing myself to heal physically because I don't know how to receive aid.

I now know that humility was the hardest lesson I had to learn. That, and the fundamental quality of caregiving. People want to help. It is how we survive as a species. I needed so much assistance, and I DO NOT ask for help. It goes against my nature; I am the caregiver. Learning how to receive care showed me all the ways I had used caregiving to keep people at a distance. I would rush in before anyone asked for help. I would co-opt the narrative by taking charge and control. I did not want to be vulnerable. Through the healing process, I learned many valuable lessons. Discovering the unhealthy way I thought I was helping people made me a better caregiver and a vastly better person. It is disrespectful to assume help is needed before being asked. This suggests people don't have their own answers, and it belittles their intelligence. Caregiving is not about solving problems; it is about being available and present when asked. It can be as simple as putting down the smartphone and focusing on the conversation at hand.

Day 14: Friday, December 30, 2022

Yesterday I crashed. I awoke feeling off and in a dark mood. I don't have words to describe how deeply I felt the weight of loss and hopelessness. The restraints of the changes to my physical life anchored me in the pit of despair. I could not pull free. I was lost to the darkness of uncertainty. I could not fight it. It was too heavy.

I cried myself awake.

After a few rough hours and visits from a couple very concerned doctors, I met with the counselor on staff here. She was very supportive and helped to explain a small piece of my journey. She said all patients crash at some point. It is part of the grieving process. Facing the fight and understanding there are no rules are necessary steps on the road to recovery. Each individual has to find a path through to the other side.

I finally let go of my expectations and attachments to unrealistic outcomes. I chose to simply live the day as it unfolded, to live with my misery and meet myself where I was. *I accepted that I did not know how long my recovery would take.*

In the end, I had a good day of both physical and occupational therapy. I had no resistance left in me. I stopped fighting, simply accepted, and worked—humbled.

For the first time in two weeks, I no longer feel like a stranger in my own body.

Even though I was starting to recover physically, the long-term emotional effects of my near-death experience had not set in. The full reality of what I was going through was still off in the distance, waiting for me to catch up. The professionals had warned me that I was a long way from being healed and not to get ahead of myself. So much had changed, and I was struggling. I was comparing my current self to my past self. I did the rehab work and was trying to keep a positive mental attitude, but looking back at that day, it's obvious I was in a place of deep emotional conflict. On the surface I was being positive and optimistic, but I had not fully embraced the fact that I had changed. My life was being altered fundamentally, and I needed to transform to be at peace.

My view lacked personal accountability. I made many assumptions relating to both me and those around me. I took for granted that I knew the answers. Transformation brings a fresh sense of self-awareness followed by clarity. I did not give up. I listened to my body. I paid attention to what felt right and what did not make me feel anxious. Through the weeks that followed, I leaned into those thoughts and followed that direction. As I did, I began to gain confidence. I used my less-desirable qualities as a measuring stick to gauge my growth. The most important change was to develop a fundamental respect for other people. I became present in my relationships. I respected and listened. I participated in my conversations, and I stopped making assumptions about people.

Day 15: Saturday, December 31, 2022

A friend sent me a note today, reminding me to look for calm waters. I've always envisioned the depths of my soul as an endless, peaceful sea that glides with a gentle, rhythmic movement. It's like a barometer offering me an awareness of my inner self. Therefore, I walk and meditate. The gentle cadence coalesces into a synchronizing of body and mind. This opens me up to hearing my authentic self, the voice buried under the constant bombardment of life's daily grind. I can only sense this voice, the true me, for a few seconds. It is profoundly illuminating, and it guides my day to a proper perspective. Over time, these few seconds of awareness grow into a sense of integrity, character, and values. These little steps create a path and give me strength to step into an unknown future.

Today, I am grasping to find that rhythm without walking. It is much harder. I am constantly battling a new voice that cries out, "Why me? Why did this happen to me?" (Simple, blind acceptance of where I am is currently my only counterbalance.) Yet I am having successes.

My recovery time is an opportunity to grow. I am opening myself to think differently. I suddenly have time to explore new directions. I can create new pathways to share my voice, my vision, and my story.

I'm learning to focus on what brings me joy.

Reading these posts, I am aware of the daily emotional highs and lows. This is the nature of recovery. It takes time to incorporate healthy behaviors. Repetition replaces old patterns and thoughts. When I'm feeling alone and the noise in my head won't quiet, I've learned to reach out for help. The words of a friend or a caring touch can be enough to bring peace and settle my overactive mind. That connection helps me find emotional balance.

Day 16: Sunday, January 1, 2023

A few random observations from a hospital bed.

1. In the past seven days, I've showered in front of five different women—and didn't make a dime.
2. Making a joke about ordering a servant bell from Amazon.com went over badly.
3. My attempt to get a prescription for sponge baths: unsuccessful.
4. Randomly asking for a middle-of-the-night foot massage: Nope
5. Hospital gowns are not meant to be worn in the wind.
6. It's OK to ask for help when one's pants are falling down.
7. When relearning to use a kitchen, any comments on its cleanliness could make for more occupational therapy in the form of scrubbing.

8. Hospital beds have loud break alarms. (I'll let you ponder on how I figured that one out. I'd love to hear your thoughts.)

9. Morning rush hour on the rehab floor is waiting for somebody to walk me to the bathroom.

10. On this floor, the volume on every TV is stuck at 11 (because 11 is louder than 10).

This day was hard for me. The start of a new year and the plans I made for my future were all in doubt. Everything, every idea, was replaced with precarious uncertainty. I was overwhelmed with too many questions and no answers. I hate to say this: I didn't want to write a reflection about this day. I'd have to admit to you my use of humor was a means of deflecting from my feelings of anxiety. I tried to "roll" with my experience in the hospital, but it was hard. I went to sleep every night fearing I would not wake the next day. Or that I'd never walk again. I was scared. Even today, months later, I am scared I could relapse. (My doctor assures me that's not possible. But it still floats into my consciousness occasionally.) Reading this post reminds me of those early days in my recovery.

Day 17: Monday, January 2, 2023

I slept a deep, healing sleep. I have finally accepted and found peace with the healing process. At least for today.

I had been afraid to sleep. I think I wanted to be awake to feel my body. For the past two weeks, I've felt like a passenger on a steam train chugging across frozen Siberia, grasping to hold myself upright while sitting on an uncomfortable, worn, wooden bench. A passenger with no control over the destination.

The worst part is waking up. There's a knitting-needle-sized poke of awareness that reminds me that I can't just jump out of bed. My day begins with halting steps, reminding me I have not yet healed.

When I started rehab, I was told that after two weeks, I could probably move about using a walker. I thought "F--- that! I'm gonna walk out of here." I'm still using a walker. It's humbling to accept that I'm not in control. There are facets of recovery that are simply physiological, the way a body normally functions, and these take time to heal.

Every day I watch the sunrise. I go through my meditative process and find my balance. A simple affirmation of life is all I need to set my feet on the best path. It is truly an uncommon road.

I am slowly recovering. I have sixty-five percent range of motion with my left arm, but it's only about twenty percent of its original strength. I can lift my left leg. And if I focus and concentrate, I can move my left toes a tiny bit. I can now shuffle using a walker, but after 100 or so steps, I'm fried.

This day stands out as one of the most important of my life. I moved my left toes. Well, I twitched them, maybe a millimeter. But I moved those little insignificant digits. I had silently made a pact with myself that if I could move my toes again, I would get my life back. Every morning as I lay in my hospital bed, I strained and focused all my might to feel them move. Finally, after two weeks of trying, they twitched. I knew I'd be OK. I knew I would walk out of the hospital.

Day 18: Tuesday, January 3, 2023

I want to share a few great moments with all of you.

I am trying hard: working out, building strength, creating muscle memory, and resting my body and brain. I'm weak, and I tire quickly. Aside from the physical challenges, I catch myself daily standing waist deep in an emotional mud pit. Day to day, even hour to hour, small victories give way to the physical limitations of my body. Without the support of my physical therapists, who remind me these setbacks are my body giving me feedback, I'd sink into despair. I asked my PTs to push me. Now I know my limitations and how hard I can work. But all the efforts are paying off.

Today I felt myself progressing instead of simply surviving the process. My confidence was much higher than it's been since the stroke. A lot of my sense of wellbeing has to do with the physical work I'm doing, but some is from the blood reabsorbing into my body. My brain is making connections again.

I've been struggling with the walker. For me to walk, I must concentrate on many bits and pieces working together. It's not natural anymore. To move the walker, I have to use my left arm and at the same time tighten my glutes, keep my toe up, lift my foot, and take a successful step. It's not intuitive or instinctive. If I'm concentrating on walking and I talk to somebody, I stumble. There's just not enough bandwidth in my head to do it all.

I decided to try a cane instead. What a difference! By taking my left arm out of the equation, I was able to focus more of my energy on walking properly. For the first time in nearly three weeks, I felt I was in my body again. We worked all afternoon on cane walking techniques. I am so excited! At the end of the day, I've been given permission to walk with a cane. I am literally taking the first steps toward regaining my old life.

To write these words, I've had to live these experiences.

I woke up that morning and decided I was going to walk. Just like that, I had made up my mind. I would walk out of the hospital and into the rest of my life. I set my mind to the task; I knew I could walk! I could wiggle my toes, so I could walk. This is an example of having the right mindset and intentions. I set a personal goal of moving my toes. When I did, I believed I could walk, and I did. Looking back now and rereading this post brings tears to my eyes. Even now, I consider that day transformative. That moment was the turning point. It was when I knew, when I truly believed, I would make a full recovery. That day set me free.

I relied on friends and family to get me out of my hospital room. These short trips around the complex were a nice change of scenery but frustrated me because I wanted to heal faster.

Day 19: Wednesday, January 4, 2023

I've had a bunch of internal conversations regarding the idea of transformation. I'm never the person I was yesterday. And tomorrow I'll be a twenty-four-hour upgrade on today's model. My current path brings a different facet to my life, and it's going to transform me in unexpected directions. It's forcing me to grow, and it's revealing new potential.

I've been presented (I choose to see it this way) with the opportunity to experience life with a different perspective. I've had to reassess who I am in the physical world. (Am I that man I see in the mirror? Wait, when did I lose my hair and go gray?) I recognize much of my self-awareness was and is connected to my physical vessel.

The past three weeks were, by far, the most humbling of my life. I've had to rely on help to do just about everything. My calves still have the muscle retention of Jell-O (not what I wanted to see in the mirror). When a person loses his eyesight, he learns to trust his other senses to navigate his way through life. My self-worth, within the confines of this diminished body, had to be reexamined. The old rules of how I lived my life do not apply to this Steve. Realizing this broke me down to my core, and I learned that I must appreciate who I am today. I let go of who I was and accepted the possibility of a new version I did not yet know. From this small but poignant emotional shift, I had a chance to reboot. I reevaluated and readjusted not only

My left foot dragged, hindering my ability to walk. My doctors ordered a custom-made ankle brace to keep my toes pointed up to help retrain my muscles.

my expectations but also how I judged my personal history. I had always used the "less successful" moments of my life as a means to minimize my dreams and desires. I let the fear of failure hold me back. I realized I had defined "failure" as not meeting what I thought others expected of me. When I carefully looked at my life, I've learned and grown and improved. I am a better version every day.

Gazing over the wall of my personal garden, I'm discovering an alluring estate. Planted throughout my lifetime, seedlings have matured. As I crack open the gate, I'm awash with colorful insights and subtle nuances of unexpected beauty. My efforts to live a purposeful life with proper intentions have cultivated the fertile landscape of my personality. With great satisfaction, I see with a new perspective that my desire to grow into an enlightened person does not solely rely on my physical capabilities.

Even with a lifetime of missteps and regrets, I trust that I've chosen a good life and that is showing up in positive ways. This attitude gives me the insight to live life in such a way that the physical vessel is less important.

I choose, even on the best of days, to live a joyful life.

I was deeply introspective as I tried to process the previous weeks. So many days along my journey have ended with a profound sense of self-awareness bubbling to the surface of my consciousness. As I reread these entries from the early days of my recovery, I am still moved and feel there is so much more that must be explored.

Day 20: Thursday, January 5, 2023

All my focus was on ten. Ten terrifying steps.

I was discharged yesterday from the in-hospital rehab unit, an environment designed to keep patients safe. I was mentally and physically drained as I maneuvered through the real world, where personal safety is largely left to the individual and once-routine activities can suddenly become precarious.

One of my rehab goals was to move successfully and safely within the walls of a friend's house. She graciously allowed me to stay with her while I did my outpatient rehab. But there were ten steps to the entrance.

I faced the ten. I'd been "training" for that challenge. As I stood at the base of the stairs, I was almost spent. The simple act of traveling to my friend's house wore me out. Looping in my head was the voice of Clare Torry singing on Pink Floyd's "The Great Gig in the Sky." Her voice cried out the raw emotions at the edge of the abyss of the unknown.

Focusing on taking each step required all my energy. The rules of navigating, the tiny adjustments we make to safely move through the world, were no longer instinctual and required all my attention, destabilizing me. My hospital world was set up to support my strengths; the real world ain't that. I felt how weak and inadequate my body was again. It was a serious reality check.

I love challenges. Usually when I face them, I have everything at my disposal, my full mental and physical toolbox. At this point, I could go into detail about how each step was a mountain, but I'm not writing crumpled at the base of the stairs. Climbing those ten little steps was one of the hardest tasks I've faced in my life. While in the hospital, I even had anxiety dreams about the challenge. After the drain of that nasty climb, I went straight to bed and slept for two hours. Ten steps and I was physically and emotionally spent.

A few years ago, I read a story about astronauts returning to Earth after an extended time on the international space station. The article focused on the challenges the astronauts faced when relearning to walk after so long in a weightless environment. Today I can seriously relate to the emotional and physical stress an astronaut faces when returning to Earth.

Stairs, any stairs, still make me pause. I stop and calculate the danger. I know I am at the greatest risk when climbing. I set my intention and determined a strategy. How will I start? Which foot first? What can I hang onto if I miss a step? I prepare. I have had to learn to slow down and to accept the adjustments I must make to live my life safely.

Day 21: Friday, January 6, 2023

Today I'm giving in and acknowledging that I need to rest. Today is the start of my third week on this journey. As much as I wish I could come up with some profound statement or in-depth look at myself, I'm just tired. My brain is fried. My body needs to heal.

I feel envious. My friends in Florida are starting their art fair season without me. It's hard because so much of my identity is wrapped up in sharing and selling my work. As you may know, I sell my photographs at art fairs. I usually spend the winter in Florida selling my work. It is a robust art fair season. I make half my annual income in the first quarter of the year in Florida. Honestly, I know I cannot take on the challenge of an art fair. I know the physical and mental demands, and I am nowhere near capable of that kind of undertaking. But because I know, I have a clear goal to work toward.

I had cabin fever from being stuck in my small hospital room, and I was ready to get out. I assumed my days would be a slightly less convenient version of my pre-stroke life. I was wrong. Very wrong. My hospital stay was set up for safety and success. I felt very confident there. Nothing in the outside world was geared toward my needs. That first day out was one of the hardest I've ever experienced. Navigating curbs and endless uneven surfaces took all my concentration. And I still had to climb those ten steps.

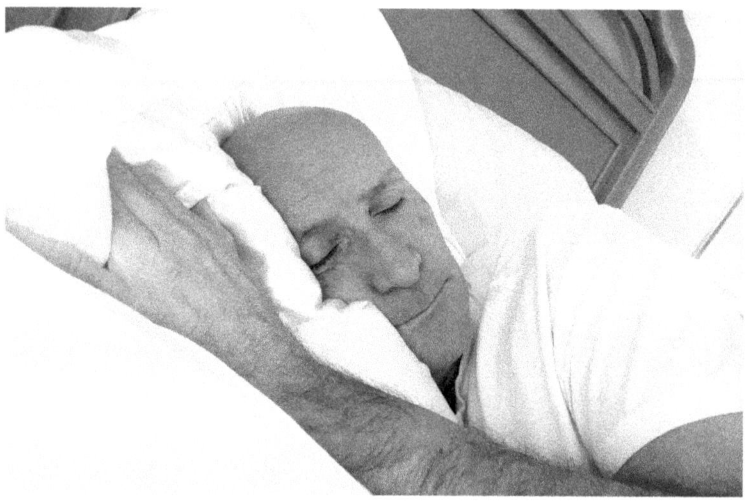

I was unrealistic about what I could accomplish after my hospital release. I pushed myself to be "normal" and felt guilty about needing so much rest. My body needed time to recover and heal. I learned to temper my expectations and found solace in small victories.

In the past, I walked without any conscious thought to my movements. My steps were instinctive. At this point in my recovery, I still had to think about the individual parts of walking—the order of muscle motions and where to place my feet. I had to plan my actions and think very strategically. Each step needed my full concentration. I was as tired in twenty minutes as I felt after a full day of rehab. The weariness of that day and many days after taught me to listen to my body. When I need to stop, I stop. Rest and reset. Some lessons must be lived to be learned.

Day 22: Saturday, January 7, 2023

I believe that an inactive body leads to an inactive mind. My most profound moments of awareness, the ones that truly impact how I see and understand myself, have all come while I was walking and meditating.

As I slowly gain control over my body, I feel the need to expand. My friend and I are taking daily "field trips." Running errands. Yep, I'm descending and climbing the ten steps, still with a huge amount of caution. I have a profound understanding of the physical challenges I face with each outing. After walking the length of about two football fields, I shake with exhaustion. My limitations, although monumental to me, are nothing compared to what so many others face.

I am gaining more confidence walking every day as I test and then push my limits. I've had some success, but … well, let's just say I'm not ready to leap into bed. (Thank God for soft landings.)

To become good at something, you reproduce that experience over and over until eventually it conditions your mind and body to work as one. The idea is to do it so often that you don't even think about it. It becomes subconscious. That is when you've mastered the ability.

I didn't want to sit at home, replacing one small space with another. I believed that the best way to improve physically was to take on the challenges of living a normal life. My endurance was meager compared to a healthy person's. Eventually I realized I could not keep up with my friends. And by not voicing my needs, I was perpetuating their assumptions that I could. I needed a lot of rest, so I developed a rhythm of activity and rest that gave me the downtime I needed and helped me gauge my recovery success.

Day 23: Sunday, January 8, 2023

Our life paths are made up of multiple interwoven storylines. When gathered, they tell our tale. Each of these threads takes energy. Each needs nurturing and nourishment. Some are hidden or buried. Others demand our attention and exact a tremendous amount of mental information. Focus too much energy into one story, and others are neglected and fray.

Knowing which storylines to focus your energy on goes hand-in-hand with recognizing your goals and values. Think in terms of time. If you waste time with unproductive thoughts, you abandon satisfying and productive storylines. By letting go of unworthy thoughts, you free your mind to focus elsewhere.

I have found that by minimizing my mental distractions, I can comfortably and gracefully appreciate aspects of my life that need nurturing. I am open to the possibilities of what can be. I had been using vast amounts of mental energy to manage my future, planning for every and all possible occurrences. Multiple threads never found their way into my life. It's as if I were weaving an alternative fabric. It was using so much of my energy that I had almost nothing left for the real me. It is like telling a lie. Once spoken, it must be managed. Eventually it takes on a life of its own. Having a stroke has changed the path of my life and given me clarity. My recovery needs have pushed aside many distractions. I simply do not have to deal with them. I recognize my needs—my real needs, not the fabrications crafted to fit into a possible future.

I continue to peruse this path of self-awareness. My knowledge of unhealthy thoughts, of which I have many, is expanding. I wrote earlier about listening to my body's response to internal questions. Over time I have learned to trust this and lean into the answers that feel right. It's possible to find balance while managing the past, living in the present, and having goals for the future.

Day 24: Monday, January 9, 2023

If weeds take root in your mental garden, they can choke out more productive seedlings. Plant kernels of positive, confidence-building thoughts. Feed them with your values and intentions. It all comes down to what you nurture. Eventually your garden will grow to be a robust, vibrant, living aspect of your personality.

I had doubts this morning, nagging fears and anxiety. The weeds had sprouted. I explored how these feelings entered my thoughts. Ultimately, I realized it was fear of the unknown. So much had changed in the past month. I had let my mind wander, and I had drifted off course. I needed to readjust.

The process of recovering from a stroke starts with finding small, achievable successes. Every morning, I struggled to put on my own socks. This was one of the simple life skills that had to be mastered if I ever wanted to leave the hospital. The first few days I needed help, but eventually I figured out a way to wedge my left foot into a pillow on my bed to hold it steady. I'd lift my left leg with my right hand. I could get the sock around my toes, and use my right hand and pull with my back to tug it over my foot and heel. What had once been a matter of simple routine, putting on socks, became a daily achievement. Recognizing these small successes as an accounting of my efforts, overcoming the daily challenges, became a record of my progress.

I stopped comparing my current self to my pre-stroke self. Instead, I looked at yesterday's version as a guide. Had I made progress? Did I have greater endurance yesterday than a week ago? I learned to measure my physical improvements day to day, instead of comparing my progress to the person I was six months or a year ago.

Emotionally, acceptance is paramount. I did not do this to myself. I did not intend to have a stroke. It just happened to me. I know this is a huge life transformative adjustment, but realizing I am not at fault is key to moving forward. The journey of recovery is made from small steps.

I began very intensive outpatient rehab today. The plan calls for retraining my body for six hours per day. I have never worked so hard in my life. I've had plenty of strenuous days, but I had full control over my body. Today was an assessment day. My physical therapy team needed a baseline to create my recovery plan.

My primary physical therapist compelled me to walk without my cane. "Are you sure?" I asked. She nodded confidently, which gave me the courage to try. In less than a week, my self-assurance and physical growth allowed me to go from a walker to a cane to free walking. Strength-wise, it's not safe for me to go on uneven surfaces or to go far, but it's a start.

We live the life we make for ourselves.

I realized a few years ago I was not happy with my life. I was not depressed, just unsatisfied with where I was going. And I don't have any huge regrets. I don't maliciously harm anyone. I was living a good and honorable life; one I am proud to own. What was the conflict?

I asked myself an important question: What was the root of my unhappiness? After much self-evaluation, the answer emerged. I was not living for me. What I mean is I was making assumptions about what I thought was expected of me. Instead of living the authentic self, I was hoping for acceptance by fitting in. I was trying to live up to expectations that probably were not real, but in my mind, they were. I saw myself through a prism based on fear and thoughts of rejection.

Knowing the nature of my personality helps me navigate the nuances of the future. It's become easier to step into the unknown because I know where I've come from, and that gives me strength to step into an unclear future.

Day 25: Tuesday, January 10, 2023

My left leg is fried. It's so weak that I had to use my knees to crawl up the last two steps today. (Yes, those steps.) The muscles around my clavicle are burning. My hips ache deeply. But I feel emotionally energized. I'm alive. I can feel everything.

For weeks, my brain was not talking to my left side. The simplest tasks required extra hands to accomplish them. I can honestly say that even in the depths of my fear and despair, I never gave up. We humans are resilient. We survive. I fight for life. I live for challenges. A mundane, safe existence bores me. I draw strength from figuring out how to fly my kite on a windless day: Run faster. This broken body is a flat tire on the road of my life. I am not finished writing my story.

My brain is finally connected to my body. It's the strangest experience, to feel everything again. Without the neuro connection, I had no way of understanding how to use that information. The feedback loop was severed. It was an empty sensation, like when I have a cold and can't taste food. I know flavor is there; I just can't taste it. Today I can taste everything in my garden.

My muscles have been devastated by the lack of information. I must teach my brain and body how to walk again. Physical therapy is kicking my backside. I'm working hard—six hours, three days a week—because I want to walk again. I want to do my work again. I am improving rapidly. Over short distances, I'm walking somewhat confidently without a cane. It's not majestic, but I'm walking. My goal: to be able to sell my work at an art fair again in six weeks. My physical therapists are not sure about the timeline, but that's my goal.

No one ever told me I needed a recovery goal. From day one, I decided and expressed my plan to be back at work eight weeks later. I never let go of that agenda. Having goals to work toward, even in my most fearful moments, made it possible for me to believe in and accept the recovery plan and to do the work to achieve my desired outcome.

Day 26: Wednesday, January 11, 2023

I am more than what I eat and what I do; I'm also what I think.

Yesterday was the first day I had the energy to focus on doing abstract tasks. I finally dug into a persistent pile of neglected business communications. I had to check and recheck myself. Work that normally takes me forty-five minutes required over three hours to complete. My daily posts, as much as I enjoy sharing my journey, take four to five hours to complete. (I work on them throughout the day.)

Yesterday was a day of physical rest, recovery, and recuperation. My body is tired. My care providers told me the first two weeks of physical therapy would take everything out of me and work me hard. They told me to expect needing a lot of sleep and rest.

This is all I have to write for today. I have PT today. I hate to admit that my body doesn't want to go. I'm still tired. One small step….

I know now that if I did not have the professional quality of care at my rehab clinic, then I would not have recovered as fast as I did. Every day was structured for my success. The staff had a focused plan that was executed with precision. Because the schedule was grueling, I found that for the first two weeks when I was not at the clinic, I had to rest. Not only was my body tired, but I also could not focus my thoughts. Both my body and my brain needed rest. A small portion of my neural pathways needed to be rewritten. I had no choice but to rest when I was weary because I did not have complete control of my body. This was when I was at the most risk of injuring myself.

Day 27: Thursday, January 12, 2023

There's a personal place an artist speaks from that transcends the craft of the medium. It is the pure expression of the individuality of the soul. It's an artist's compulsion to share a message that goes deeper than rational thought.

To make the best art, I essentially speak from my core. I must know myself. Over the past month, I've had to look and dig deep to find a sense of integrity and purpose. This is my opportunity to reflect on my journey and what I've created throughout my lifetime.

I have wavered, zigged, zagged, and run. I've allowed distractions and hid from myself. Facing and speaking my truth meant that I had to truly accept myself and the parts of me that I'm afraid to acknowledge. No, I'm not going to list them. We all have these lists.

I started down the path of intentional, directed self-understanding long before the hemorrhage in my brain. As my physical world shrank, I realized my lifestyle had continued to enable me to run from myself. With no physical means to deflect, I've begun to embrace myself and where I am today. It is a truly remarkable moment of self-awareness.

Most importantly, I trust myself, and I accept that today I am the best version of me. Or at least the most current version. To find my purpose in life, I had to find myself.

The core of my art, regardless of how I express it, is about sharing the authenticity of my personal experiences. I create with the intention of opening an emotional connection with you. I know I am touching many lives because the light you reflect back shines with crystal clarity.

As I polish this new facet in the diamond of my life, I'm honored that you share it with me.

As I reread these entries, I am proud. I stayed focused and let the positive nature of my personality carry my resolve. It was an intentional daily exercise of self-awareness. As my brain was rewriting new pathways, I chose to consciously infuse an optimistic perspective into the process. I chose this opportunity to make changes in my attitude both toward my physical needs and my outlook on my life. I have a solid perspective on my life. I am much more consistent about how I approach my everyday thoughts. I am not trying to fit in. I am content to simply be me. I know I will make plenty of mistakes, and I am fine with not being perfect or in control of every situation. I have switched my approach from one of fear of vulnerability and emotional exposure to one of acceptance— one of finding the lessons that help shape me into a more complete and content person.

Day 28: Friday, January 13, 2023

I had so much fun last night. Friends and family came over to celebrate my birthday. We poked fun at one another and laughed at silly things. It was one of those great gatherings with no agenda. Just a simple loosening of the rules. I hobbled around like a one-legged pirate on a ship in the middle of a hurricane as I tried to show off my increasing mobility. Not once did I feel I was any less of a good host. I did tire easily, yet I felt in no way diminished. As the sun rises on a new day, I am emotionally rejuvenated. I feel normal.

Upon reflection, I can see I needed to be with friends and family. That part of the day felt normal. Yet at another level, I was not physically whole. In my post, I was very optimistic about how good I felt. But compared to where I was just a week before, I was very excited. The next day my energy crashed, and I had to rest most the day.

Day 29: Saturday, January 14, 2023

The dignity of my story can only be told by me. If I don't speak about my trauma, I will become isolated and alone. If I think I am the only one who understands my struggles, the pain becomes entrenched within my body and my mind.

Those who know me might think, "Yeah right, Steve, you spew

your feelings like a two-year-old spews snot when sneezing." But I have always chosen very carefully and measured what I share.

I am learning disabled. I've struggled my whole life to fit in with the "normal" world. All the measures of success and acceptance are built around the idea of what is quantifiable and trackable. I grew up with the message that I was somehow less-than. The system, when I was a kid, was not set up to handle people who learn differently. I hid my resentment and pain. Unknowingly, I walled myself off from my true self. I believed I was broken. I learned a different set of survival skills with the unintended result of running and hiding from myself and, by extension, everyone else in my life.

I've spent my life concealing my true disability. This may sound strange, but being physically challenged is so much easier for me emotionally. It's an observable handicap. There is an obvious reason for my struggle. Even as I write, in this moment, every impulse inside of me screams, "Shut down! Don't expose yourself to the gaze of judgment." I have to force myself to bring these words to the surface.

I've made a choice to tell my story, to share it on my terms and expose my emotional trauma and pain. I can look at it and not feel isolated. I am rewriting old habits entrenched from years of running and hiding. Instead of being mediocre while trying to "fix" my weaknesses, I shine the light on my strengths. This has become my personal mantra. I see myself as an amazing gift that gives me the ability to see the world in a way that is truly my own. I am one of one.

I've always escaped reality in the stories I told myself about me. I let my mind wander into a fantasy realm where no one can hurt me and where the light of admiration shines only on me. Having a stroke is real and tied to the world. There is no gray area to get lost in. I am in my body and tethered in the moment by necessity. As I've recovered and less of my mental energy is needed to physically function, there's a headspace in which I begin to drift into old behaviors. Unconscious habits become a means of escape. Fortunately, now I can recognize when I'm slipping and can reconcile a lifetime of escape thoughts with the need to rest my mind.

Day 30: Sunday, January 15, 2023

My physical therapist told me I am entering one of the most dangerous phases of my physical recovery: I'm getting the big muscle groups back online that dictate the large motor skills, but my fine motor skills that control the subtlety of balance and safety have not yet developed.

The instinctive movements are starting to return, but I don't have the subtle strength to move in a way that has the nuances of my old body. When I was cooking, I reached with my left arm to turn something in the hot skillet, and my arm just dropped. It touched the edge of the pan. Fortunately, it didn't burn me, but it seared into my brain that I need to be very careful.

I'm also pushing myself. I want to get out and do more. My world is very small right now, and I want it to be big again. I'm not always listening to my body. I'm physically tired. I have a full day of physical therapy today, and I don't feel as if my body is in a place to be productive.

These are lessons that I carry forward. I'm learning a new way of how to successfully manage my life. In the past, I did not have to think before I moved; now I am very aware of my limitations. I recently talked with a friend about downhill skiing, a sport I was very proficient in, and I started thinking about whether I would feel safe. I realize I will be able to ski, but I will have to take a different approach. Even if I were perfectly healthy, I could not ski like a kid again. I plan to make the adjustments needed, safely test my limits, and still enjoy the experience.

Day 31: Monday, January 16, 2023

Rehab is a wholehearted pilgrimage to visualize perfection. In other words, I know where I want to go, and getting there is an epic undertaking. It's a mind-bending reality because it's going to take me months to regain what was lost in minutes.

As I've mentioned, I attend rehab three days a week. Yesterday's sessions involved three hours of lower body, two hours of upper body, and one hour of core work, with a forty-minute lunch break mixed in. It is a total-body workout intended to get me functioning normally. Honestly, I might be fitter than I have been for at least a decade.

When I'm there, I push myself. I don't sit still. My mind always leaps out of my comfort zone, and my body follows. Yesterday I walked into rehab tired, but my confidence remained. I didn't quit. I worked. I asked to be challenged and remained dedicated.

I am sore. I think the only part of my body not growling with pain is the tip of my left pinky. I have no stamina, but I recognize that my progress is rapid. Four weeks ago, my left side was paralyzed. Over the last ten days, I've transformed. About a week ago, I was fitted for an ankle brace to help keep my left foot from dragging. I only wore it for a week. Today I don't need a walker, a cane, or an ankle brace. Today I am walking.

The process of rehab is part physical and part mental. The physical aspects are a repetitive set of focused skills designed to strengthen and test the body. In my case, I had to learn how to walk and use my arm and hand again. As part of my initial session, we talked about my goals and my lifestyle. For example, I like to cook. Part of my rehab involved how to safely use knives and the stove. I had to master each skill set's list of required abilities before I could move on to the next, more difficult set.

The mental aspect is a very personal journey. In the first few days after my stroke, I decided I would be OK with whatever I could accomplish. I was going to live life no matter the physical limitations. Therefore, I wrote every day. Writing served my need to express myself creatively. Blogging daily focused my mental energy. I wrote for hours every day. Instead of worrying about the future, I actively created positive outcomes.

Day 32: Tuesday, January 17, 2023

I had my first meeting with the staff nurse practitioner at my rehab clinic. I learned that in a few areas of recovery, I'm ahead of schedule. This went straight to my head. She also thought it would be very likely for me to travel to Florida in late February for the Naples National Art Fair. This reinforced my overreaching optimism. I tell myself constantly not to get ahead of myself, but….

As I sauntered down the hall afterward, I felt like I was the cat who caught the mouse. I threw myself into my workouts—legs, back, core. I didn't listen to my body. The mouse slipped away. I was exhausted. I'm regaining strength, but I lack the ability to carry out regular daily tasks for more than ten or fifteen minutes. Endurance is definitely something you build up to, and it can't be forced.

To drive again, I have to pass a series of standard tests. The first is a gas-pedal-to-brake timed test. I must average that maneuver in half a second. In the first attempt, I was one-tenth of a second over. The second time, I improved slightly. I averaged four-tenths of a second on my third try. I could have passed, but what became very clear to me was that I don't have the stamina to drive yet. Although I appear normal in the mirror, I am unsafe. Ego checked.

It's obvious that by pushing my physical development, I'm not taking good care of myself. Today is a day to reflect on setting realistic goals and not becoming attached to outcomes. I am humbled.

Recovery is a slow and frustrating process. Much of it is mental. I had many misguided standards of success. The lesson I missed again and again was to not compare myself to my pre-stroke self. I needed to focus on the small task-to-task, day-to-day improvements. I was aiming for perfection and judging my progress unrealistically. The only fair barometer of my success should have been whether I was doing better than the day before. I was not paying attention to my body, my stamina, and my level of exhaustion. Those were the best indicators of my progress.

Day 33: Wednesday, January 18, 2023

My original plan yesterday was to knock out a bunch of business details and to prepare for the upcoming art fair season.

Unfortunately, I slept poorly the night before. My body hurt, and I woke up throughout the night in pain. Today I had a hard time staying focused and finally gave in to the fatigue. I slept most of the day. Show prep and business correspondence would have to wait.

My only constant was the inconsistency of my recovery journey. I could not find a predictable pattern. The best measure of how I was feeling was to listen to my body. I would feel fine, and within a few minutes, I needed rest. I struggled with giving myself mental and emotional breaks. I was frustrated.

Day 34: Thursday, January 19, 2023

Yesterday I had my two-week assessment. I've made remarkable progress in some areas and only average progress in others. When moving forward, I am in good shape. Multitasking while walking still challenges me. I need most of my attention to move my body. If there is any distraction, I lose my balance. Stairs continue to be problematic. My left arm is weak and does not respond to my instinctive instructions. When I am standing still and concentrating, I can use it for most tasks, but only for a short time. I struggle with simple things like balance, counting backwards, and fatigue. For two nights, I didn't sleep well because my body aches kept waking me up. Finally, last night, I had a good night's sleep—a solid, deep sleep.

I woke up energized and alert. This morning, here at home, I went through a couple recovery assessments and nailed them.

At this point, I was just beginning to discover a rhythm to energy versus rest needs. I was pushing myself and not giving myself a respite. I was blind to the reality of recovery. I wanted to be my old self and get on with my life. But I soon realized that the harder I worked without rest, the longer the physical recovery time I needed. I found thirty minutes of any kind of work, whether physical or mental, called for an equal amount of time to rest. I settled into a pattern. Over time, I noticed I could work harder for longer periods and needed less rest. This formula helped me to more accurately evaluate my recovery progress.

Day 35: Friday, January 20, 2023

I gladly bow to the idea of a higher power, the divine, the energy of the universe. I believe in the power of prayer, the focused energy of individuals coming together and combining their intentions toward a shared goal. I don't take this lightly; I recognize its importance. I like to think all this energy is working for and with me. I feel the power influencing the direction of my life.

I have been stumbling toward my future. I believe with all my heart that I have a story to tell. It might not seem profound or earth-shattering. I'm not going to change the world. However, I have a calling, or desire, to broadcast my unique insight into life. Each one of us has a one-of-a-kind view of the world. I believe it's my "job" to share my process as I scratch away each opaque layer of mental debris on my path toward understanding.

By telling my story, I'm forced to think deeply about the connections I'm making. At times, the thoughts cascade, one leading to another, faster than I can comprehend. Certainly, faster than I can write about them. As I reach for one idea, others slip by. I could easily get lost in the flood. I am learning to hang on to one idea and explore that concept. This helps me navigate the complexities of my changing world.

My stroke has given me a deeper, more profound appreciation for life—for *my* life. Comprehending what is being revealed requires time, diligence, and patience. I lean into that goal every day. Today a new understanding glimmered into my awareness: the fundamental appreciation I have for all those around me, the friends and family who have expressed their support.

I could have died from my stroke, but I didn't. The path of life is a personal journey, but along the way, we encounter people who show us where to step and who take our hand when we stumble. With such support and care, I can revisit my passions and creative ambitions as well as take time to be grateful for this life I live.

Day 36: Saturday, January 21, 2023

Trying to answer "why me?" opens an endless loop of possibilities. While lying in my hospital bed, I briefly pondered this question. At first, I felt as if I were losing control of my life. In those early days, I struggled to maintain a sense of purpose and understanding. I turned inward and looked at my life and values and goals. I have, for the most part, lived a life that makes me proud.

Asking "why?" seemed pointless. Asking "why?" is about time-traveling to the past. Seeking answers to questions relating to yesterday meant I wasn't living in the present. I've wasted too much of my life worrying about the past. And there's absolutely nothing I can do about it. Accept it, and move on! I am not giving up on my goals and dreams; I simply need to think about how to achieve them by using a different roadmap. Asking "why?" meant staring in the rearview mirror and not paying attention to the road in front of me.

Instead, I ask, "what?": What do I want my life to look like? What can I do to live where I am today? I ask myself these questions every day and will continue to ask them even when I'm back to one hundred percent.

In the early days of my recovery, my life looked as if I would require twenty-four-hour care, and I had to make peace with that reality. We change every day. We don't realize it because, for the most part, our physical changes are incremental. These readjustments usually seem glacial, but they eventually influence the outcomes of our goals. My change was more like an avalanche. When I began asking "what?" I realized my goals were still the same. The only difference was the means of transportation. Would I have a heathy body or navigate my future with an impaired one? Either way, my outlook is the same. This is important. Letting go of the past frees me to continue living my life. Adjusting does not mean a total course change.

I am certain that my speedy improvement had everything to do with my attitude. I was never going to give up on my life. "What?" is a blueprint for the future. Asking "what?" empowers me to shape my life.

I now understand that I have the ability to shape my future. I set intentions to live the life I want. By making choices today with potential goals in mind, I have a solid foundation to take on life's challenges. I fully expect to get smacked by the random nature of life's upending my plans, but because I have an objective map, I can chart my way back to my path.

The decisions we make today shape our life stories. There is no beginning and there is no end: life is a web of possibilities.

I write a lot about making healthy choices. At the most basic level, I had to take a leap of faith regarding my self-worth. A piece of that is accepting or coming to terms with myself as a person. The extent of my injury isolated me from external influences that shaped my self-esteem. Without that constant influence, the energy I dumped into managing those expectations found a healthier destination. To say it another way, that energy was no longer colored by external expectations. I learned that I could decide whether and when I care about what people think of me. Being isolated and cut off from those thoughts freed my mind to focus on me. I was not unhappy, but I was not content either. I took the time to reevaluate where I was going and what I wanted to achieve. I pointed myself in a healthier direction. I was able to see the facets of myself that I liked, and I now understand the sides I thought of as negatives are pieces of what make me, me.

Day 37: Sunday, January 22, 2023

I walked for forty minutes today. Yesterday, I walked for twenty-five minutes. My goal is to walk five miles in sixty minutes. I am slowly building endurance and stamina. The days I don't have physical therapy, I walk around the golf course near where I am staying. Even though it is winter, I walk. I like the challenge of the complex surfaces even though the mental concentration needed to navigate the path wears me out. I spent the rest of the day lying on the couch, watching football, and eating pizza. Oh well.

Being dyslexic, I learn differently. And as a person, I generally interpret the world in my own way. But I am a product of the

American educational system. When I was a kid in the public schools, no allowances were made for alternative learning styles. I was usually told I was not working hard enough. That has manifested in feeling as if I am never good enough. I feel the necessity to prove I am worthy. At this point in my life, I intellectually understand there is no supernatural being keeping tabs. It does not matter. I always feel a voice in my head reminding me that I am somehow lacking. Accepting and admitting to myself that I need downtime has been a challenge. As my maneuverability improves, I have learned to pay attention to my recuperative needs. This includes recognizing when the voice in my head is harmful.

Day 38: Monday, January 23, 2023

Yesterday I met with my physical therapy team. We talked about my progress, rehab goals, and an exit strategy. Yes, you heard me; an exit plan is in place.

I still have areas that need improvement, but I am almost ready to live independently. I must think strategically about every move. This includes the small life skills, like safely setting up my work area when cooking, and the big moves, such as determining how I will navigate through life for the next six to eight months. I have to make a living, and that requires endurance and strength. For example, I cannot build my art fair booth without help. I need to think about my show schedule and my support plan. I am fiercely independent, but I am learning how to ask for help.

I have a fixed end date, which is February 17. That's when my insurance runs out. (I just learned this yesterday.) Because my recovery has been speedy, I expect I will be ready to live independently.

I was shocked to learn I owed nearly $28,000 for rehab. Get insurance quotes in writing! I was told I was fully covered, but months later, I received a massive bill. After weeks of back-and-forth with my rehab center and the insurance company, I discovered I was not covered. My rehab clinic got a verbal quote, but when it came time to pay, the insurance company had no record of the conversation. Fortunately, my clinic came through and negotiated with me, reducing my bill to "only" $10,000.

Day 39: Tuesday, January 24, 2023

If you obsess over something, it will break your nerve.

The blue, cold "what if?" thought doesn't seep in around the gaps in my mental door frame; it kicks it off its hinges! What if this happens again? What if something else goes wrong? What if? What if? What if?

It's amazing how dropping one word from that phrase can change the equation. Asking myself what I want my life to look like is much more positive and actionable than wondering whether something else will happen. The form of the question can change my outlook.

In truth, every decision, at any moment, changes my life. There's no way around it. Pushing back, closing that "what if" door takes a positive attitude and a desire to live fearlessly. Most important is living a good life shared with amazing people. When "what if" inches into my mind, I remember all the wonderful people in my life, and I can live with that.

Recovery is cyclical. The post-traumatic stress of such an experience manifests in countless ways. The reality is that my days are filled with fear of the unknown. I have days when I am ready to address the challenges, days when I choose to push back the fear, and days when I feel helpless to the onerous effort needed to stay positive. I lean on friends for stability and have a process of recounting the numerous positive gains I've made when the burden of fear and failure inches into my psyche.

Day 40: Wednesday, January 25, 2023

Yesterday was, well, normal. I had good endurance. At the end of the day, I didn't feel like cooked egg noodles. I felt a normal level of tiredness. I cleaned the kitchen without any issues. I worked a full day. I went to a doctor's appointment, and I walked home. It was about one-half mile round trip. I had to cross a major road, which was intimidating but normal. My friends and I piled into the car and went to the grocery store. Normal! I ordered a new iPhone 14 pro. There's nothing wrong with my old phone; I just wanted to do something special for myself (I'm excited to play with the new camera). That, for me, is normal.

The simplicity of everyday normal is the sunlight after weeks of gray, cloudy days: so uncomplicated yet awakeningly brilliant. At some point, I won't think about how special "normal" feels. Today is rich with pride, accomplishment, and excitement for the future because it feels so normal.

Looking back, that normal was still a very restricted version of true normal. I did not know it then, but I still had a long way to go in recovery. It was an emotionally positive day. The thoughts of my stroke, recovery, and potential setbacks were pushed aside that day.

Day 41: Thursday, January 26, 2023

The quality of your life depends on
the quality of your thoughts.
—*Marcus Aurelias*

Rehab kicked my butt yesterday. I worked on strengthening and stretching my core and lower body. Those big muscle groups, the ones I use to walk, are screaming this morning.

I planned to walk today with the sunrise. And I could have—seriously, I could have—but I wimped out. Not because my body resisted but because the temperature was only 17°F. My snowbird blood is way too thin for this cold. (I Winter in Florida. I have a tiny house in the country about fifty miles from Fort Myers.) It occurred to me that mall walking might be my future. Instead of taking my outdoor walk, I stood on the porch, my feet bare to experience the sensation, and took my morning picture. For weeks I had been unable to sense my left foot, and briefly standing in the bitter cold, admiring the morning light, helped me feel alive.

About five years ago, I chose to live with fewer physical distractions. I was stressed. I had so many things demanding my attention that I had no time for myself. I had cars and a studio and my photography business. That meant I had all the responsibility on my shoulders. We all have burdens, but I discovered I am happiest and the most creative when my mind is free from distractions.

I decided to sell everything. I downsized, decluttered, and minimized my life. I bought a small motorhome and began traveling America. After five years of travel and a blown engine, I sold my RV and bought two tiny houses. I keep one in Wisconsin and the other in

Florida. Through this journey, I concluded stuff does not matter. In the end, at my end, everything I've accumulated is just junk someone will have to dispose of. Life for me is about experiences and memories. Going through a hemorrhagic stroke and recovery is incredibly hard. But when I think of it in terms of the personal growth and the boundless experiences, I realize my life is richer and fuller.

Day 42: Friday, January 27, 2023

I am entering a phase of recovery when I need medical rechecks. Over the next few weeks, I have follow-up appointments in cardiology, neurology, and so forth. Yesterday I had a cardio stress test. I passed. My heart is beating to the rhythm of life without concern. I don't see why I would not pass all these assessments, but the thought of a new problem surfacing scares me a little bit.

I've had the same primary doctor for decades whom I trust with every aspect of my medical life. I had so many new doctors throughout my recovery. I could not make a personal connection with any of them. It was not a question of professionalism. My care was fantastic. My first few days in the hospital, I was scared, and the hospital staff was my lifeline. But I felt like I had to simply accept their assessments, and I needed someone to see the overall situation. My primary could not advise because he was in Minnesota, and I was in Chicago. He did not have the state privileges to care for me. Once I was living on my own, I made an appointment with him and sent him all my medical records. He was the voice I needed.

Day 43: Saturday, January 28, 2023

It's a snow day—too bad it's the weekend!

When I was a kid growing up in the mountains, we had deep, deep snowfalls. I loved running in the woods with my dog. I could be 100 yards from my house, and I felt like I was transported into a realm filled with mysteries and magic. The quarter-sized snowflakes blocked out the world. It was so quiet. I could only hear my breath and my dog running beside me. I could yell as loud as I wanted, and the sound barely reached my ears. I would jump off twelve-foot-high cliffs and grab the tops of trees and swing down in the deep piles of snow. Oh, to be a teenage boy again!

Today I took two walks as the snow fell. It's a time when the sound and the light are almost the same quality: soft and muffled. I find it really hard to photograph in these conditions. I am an atmospheric-driven, visual person. Something about the edges of the light really excites me creatively. Snowy, low-light days have no edges, but I love walking into the heart of them.

It's hard to imagine that just six weeks ago I couldn't walk.

These are the thoughts that accompany me on this snowy day:

memories of a child swinging in the trees and the musings of a grown man appreciating life from a very different perspective.

As I found my footing in my life, I took the time to appreciate what I almost lost. It's sad that I had to nearly die to reacquire the richness of life. I am surrounded by beauty, and I capture it daily with my camera. Now I try to feel it with every breath.

Day 44: Sunday, January 29, 2023

I've been thinking about when my narrative ends; not my grand life tale, but my recovery story. In the first few weeks of posting, I needed a safe outlet to direct my creative energies and, more importantly, a place where I could look at the emotional roller coaster of healing a broken body. Writing gave me a microscope to examine the physical and mental difficulties I was struggling to understand.

Now, weeks later, my life is routine. Rather, I have a routine. The trauma has receded into the background, and an optimistic view of my future has surfaced.

The next phase of my life is going to be very interesting. My physical world is dropping back into a known pattern. At a much deeper level, this experience has changed me. I wish I could say I have a new … insert cliché here: "appreciation," "faith in," "understanding of" … the list goes on. Somewhere inside me, I am fundamentally different. I'm not talking about the obvious physical changes but the ones that are much deeper. Understanding those differences will take time and introspection. I don't want a chiseled-in-stone plan. I need to allow this new understanding to come forward naturally. I'm excited for the next phase of my life. Eventually, capturing images will take over my creative landscape. But for now, I'm going to keep writing.

Even now, months after I wrote this passage, I am still discovering the emotional changes I am experiencing. Suffering trauma has changed me deeply. It has changed the direction of my life. I used to continually worry about what other people thought of me. I realized no one can understand what I have gone through. This led me to the awareness that no one could ever have understood me or my life. Ever. Even before my stroke, I was unique. One of one within billions of individuals. I found self-respect. Fighting my way through the physical limitations gave me the courage to risk being myself. It is not so much that I don't care what people think; it is that I value my opinion more. I am doing what is good for me and following what makes sense in my life and for my goals.

Day 45: Monday, January 30, 2023

The Work Hardening of Steve W.

On my first day of rehab, my occupational therapist and I discussed the physical requirements of running an art fair business, which involves lugging in and setting up my booth, installing walls, hanging work, and so on.

My team has designed a new and ingenious workout routine to get me ready to go back to work.

They named that routine "Work Hardening—Steve W." It's a list of twenty exercises to perform daily to help with the demands of life on the road as an artist. As I plowed into the routine, I faced more than physical challenges. Emotionally preparing for an independent life, which I had pushed to the background, began forcing its way forward. I have to admit the thought of being on my own is both a goal and a fear.

Back to the workout. At number ten, I was tired. At fifteen, I was looking for excuses to go easy. At twenty, I was fried, and my body screamed. Nevertheless, I did it. It took all day, but I did it. I am proud! I get to do it again tomorrow.

At the end of the day, I left on wobbly legs. I could see the end, but I knew I would have many, many steps ahead to reach a better version of the work-hardened Steve W. I returned home, stepped on the ice, and slid onto my backside, reminding me that I was not my old self

I walked every day, slowly increasing the distances I covered. I had yet to learn the lesson of staying focused. My body would not respond instinctively, and mental lapses could put me in danger, such as when I slipped on the ice.

and I needed to stay focused on safety. My smile remained on my face despite my fall. Perhaps it was frozen on; the temperature was -3°F.

I laid on the ice, flat on my back. The first thoughts through my mind were, "Did I hurt myself? Did I reinjure myself? Can I move my toes?" Then I looked around to see whether anyone saw me fall. An old habit. "Do I look like a jackass, and is anyone going to laugh at me?" That led me to chuckle. I know how to walk on the ice. I grew up around ice rinks. I was thinking about the twenty or so steps ahead of me and not the threat in front of me. My first rule: stay present, which includes watching where I step.

Day 46: Tuesday, January 31, 2023

I'm shifting my mental energy from recovery thoughts to my introspective, creative voice. Deep in the physical recovery process, I needed to focus my energy on regaining what I lost. Yesterday I walked for an hour on the treadmill. I am physically improving. As I need less energy to manage my body, my mind has begun to drift into a meditative disposition. For the first time in weeks, I was able to step into an emotionally clear, meditative mindset.

As I walked, I found my rhythm. Walking helps quiet my mind. My breathing sets the tone as my stride matches and aligns with my thought patterns. I dampened the external noise and suppressed the stories I tell myself. My thoughts about the past or the future evaporated. I was left with, well, me. I like me. But I don't know myself as I did before. I am trying to figure out how this new Steve fits into old Steve's world. My goals have not changed, but how I get there is unclear. Before I was trapped by my outcomes and my desire to prove my worth to myself. I see that now.

Every day, life tosses us a new set of game pieces. How we play the game is determined by who we are and our values. How I play the game now is going to be different because I am different. I don't yet know how to express the changes. I know it is there, just under the surface. It's both unnerving and exciting.

I believe change is inevitable and life is going to happen to me. I have no control over what occurs, but I can determine the outcome. Through my actions and living with a set of personal values, I believe I can determine my future by the choices I make today.

Taking a moment to appreciate the morning sunshine. Cloudy days give me the blues.

My values are a product of my life experiences, my upbringing, and my unique brain. Living through a life-transforming event didn't change my values. It stripped away the external clutter and emotional baggage from years of misreading almost every life situation. I now have a transparent understanding of my values. I live with clearer intentions and goals. I survived a stroke. That process has given me an understanding of what I appreciate. I focused on my recovery and did not think about the external voices. Without those influencing my thoughts, I found the strength to trust and believe in my potential.

Day 47: Wednesday, February 1, 2023

Jumped out of bed in a panic. Woke up late. Running behind. I was in my head a lot last night. Didn't sleep as deeply as needed. It is almost impossible to keep the "what if" voices in check. And sometimes I just have to accept the dark thoughts and live the fear to move through it. I wish I had sage advice, but anxiety, even panic, is part of the journey. These random thoughts, for me, are nearer the surface at night.

Called an Uber for a ride to PT. On my way.

I have a strategy for compensating my rough emotional moments. I list my accomplishments, check my financial situation, think of my amazing friends, and so on. What I have found the most helpful is voicing my concerns—actually saying them out loud. And again, out loud, I use my name and ask myself how I am feeling. Voicing my concerns quiets the fear-based voices in my head.

I was not medically cleared to drive, so I called on drivers to experience independence.

Day 48: Thursday, February 2, 2023

Zip! Zing! Bang! The BIG news: I am officially done with rehab. In just under seven weeks, I went from paralyzed on my left side to a functioning middle-aged guy. I have met my goal. I will head back to Florida soon to show my work at an art fair in Naples.

I still have months of self-directed rehab and up to a year before I'm back to one hundred percent. For the past seven weeks, I've had an amazing team of specialists supporting every step of my recovery. I felt safe and had a path toward a goal. Today, my care sits on my shoulders alone.

My physical challenges are manageable. I know I am ready, and I have a plan to continue my rehab on my own. But I have this fear rolling around inside of me. What if I fail or what if something new goes wrong? The "what if?" questions have nudged their way into my thoughts. There are so many unknowns.

Honestly, I must move on with my life. Even when I was healthy, I faced countless undefined hurdles. Suffering a stroke brought to the surface the potential life-threatening obstacles and highlighted my fears. When I had a care team behind me, I felt safe. Learning how to manage my fears and structure a plan for the rest of my recovery will help. Mostly, I need to stay in the moment. Worrying about a possible future is wasted energy—energy I need to focus on my recovery.

The last day of rehab was a significant milestone. I was proud of what I had accomplished. I still am. It represented how far I had come, and I now carry a sense of achievement as I plan my life after my stroke.

Day 49: Friday, February 3, 2023

My dad wrote this note yesterday morning: "Congratulations, Steve. Mom, in spirit, and I are proud of you."

These eleven words first took my breath away, and then the tears fell. They kept pouring out. I sobbed in my friend's embrace until I quieted. Raw emotions avalanched into the deep, isolated valley of my consciousness. After nearly two months of holding it together, I finally gave in.

My mom passed away long ago. There have been many times I've turned to her memory for guidance. She has been with me through my greatest accomplishments of raising two amazing boys and receiving accolades for my work. I am proud to be the child of my parents, to be the son of MaryAnn. My first morning in the hospital, feeling scared, lost, and painfully vulnerable, I needed her. I wrapped myself in her memory. I needed the one person who I knew saw me unconditionally.

The word "Mom," shattered my resolve. I didn't have the energy to hold back two months of bridled intensity. Emotionally,

A letter from my dad reminded me how much I missed the support of my mom.

I felt like a wet rag that was twisted and contorted until every drop was squeezed out. I had no direction for my emotions. I simply needed to release and empty.

I hadn't known how much I was holding in until this great flood of tears. These weeks have been the hardest, most frightening time of my life. I've stood with a stony resilience and most days face it without flinching.

Letting go is scrubbing my soul as clean as a pristine whiteboard. I think I will use lots of bright-colored markers to illuminate the next phase of my life. I need unblemished room to write because the lessons keep coming. I've always seen my path as a solitary journey; however, I could not have made this transformation without an amazing group of friends. I have learned that unconditional love is freely given, and unconditional acceptance is equally rewarding.

I once again feel the clock ticking. It's not counting down; it's just the measured rhythm of my life.

There are different kinds of loss and grief. Some I have processed and moved on from. Some I carry. Reading this post, even months after I wrote it, still churns up my emotions. I had no emotional map to follow while healing. I am sure there are resources, but I was too stubborn to seek them. I recognize now that recovering from this kind of trauma should not be taken on alone. I had ample help for my obvious physical needs, but the hidden emotional ramifications require a different kind of care. I struggle with the idea of what it means to be vulnerable. It feels like a weakness. This mindset holds me back from mentally healing faster. Being truly vulnerable simply means being honest with myself, embracing aspects of me where I have the least confidence, letting go of certainty, and allowing others to help.

That note from my dad was a good release. I needed it.

Day 50: Saturday, February 4, 2023

I write short notes to myself that encapsulate the essence of what I'm feeling in any given moment. They are reminders that help shape my daily posts. I don't use most of them, so I decided to share a few with you:

It's a part of who I am now. It is a transformative chapter to my story.

If this is a test, I've passed.

Quiet your mind.

I've had a lot of time to ponder "why," and, truthfully, I don't care. It just is.

If I seek the answer to "why," I create a storyline around a narrative that is based on assumptions.

I am more than I am but less than I could be.

Fly, birdy, fly.

I had my first post-stroke headache yesterday. It freaked me out.

Communicate directly, honestly, and in a kind way.

There's a place within each of us that inspires creativity and is beyond worldly influences. It gives us the space to express our appreciation of life. It allows us to honor ourselves, our creative voices, and to celebrate our lives.

Know what you want so that you can consider your needs. If you don't decide, other people will decide for you.

I'm not fixated on what happened. I'm moving on.

People around you are reflections of how you treat them.

I could write a full post on any one of these thoughts. Read them as a collection of observations. Together they form an insight into my emotional narrative.

Day 51: Sunday, February 5, 2023

The other day I wrote, "I once again feel the clock ticking. It's not counting down; it's just the measured rhythm of my life."

In the hospital and in the early weeks of rehab, I had no clock. My life rhythm changed. At first, I had convinced myself I'd be out and about in a few days. Reality had not yet made its appearance in my messed-up head. The brain and body heal without any concern for time. Acceptance is letting go of an expectation-laden timeframe. Without the persistent ticking of my personal pocket watch, I could heal at a natural rhythm.

Now that I'm done with rehab, I feel the clock ticking again. In recovery, I saw my future as a foggy horizon. My life was on hold. Yesterday, while out walking, I felt the rhythm of my life solidly kick in to drive.

I began making plans as to what I need for my first art fair. I'll need help. Setting up a booth for the show is more than I can handle.

I'll need inventory. But how much? There are financial limitations. And let's not forget the actual amounts of time and energy I can expend. It could be overwhelming for me, but fortunately I can draw on my years of experience to guide me.

I am learning to appreciate my core values. I see myself with greater clarity. I am learning to respect myself and my thoughts. And I am aware of how I want to live my life. I imposed a lot of stress on myself. I now recognize that pattern. I am starting to understand the unhealthy way I had judged people. I am learning about fundamentally respecting others. I am discovering my personal guidelines and how they align with my core values. I don't know exactly where I'm going, but I'll know when I get there. I no longer fixate on the results.

It would have been easy to fall into old habits. They are all I have known. Before my stroke, I struggled to make life changes. I knew I was not living the life I wanted, and I was working to change. I read books about enlightenment and life choices. I made physical changes in my lifestyle. But the stroke forced a change in direction. The journey back to health taught me much about self-care and the process required to make changes. Stripping away the external influences freed me from them, and I was able to reboot and implement a new set of life skills.

Day 52: Monday, February 6, 2023

Tomorrow, I have a comprehensive follow-up with my neurologist at the stroke clinic. I assumed everything would be bright and shiny, so I purchased my ticket to Florida. I fly down this Sunday. I am excited and a bit nervous. This will be the first time in two months that I will be fully immersed in my old lifestyle and essentially living one hundred percent independently.

Most importantly, I'll get a feel for how far I've come and how much work is in front of me. I will be able to compare the present to the past. This should give me my first true assessment of my recovery's progress. I talked with friends who live nearby, and they are ready to help me transition to my daily routine. I will try to take time each day to find safe footing physically and emotionally.

This was a part of my plan from early in my recovery. I never told anyone, but I had a date in mind for when I was going to get back home. I am not sure this was a good idea. What if I had not met my expectations? It was a leap of faith. I never thought or believed I would not be on the plane.

Day 53: Tuesday, February 7, 2023

No charts. No maps. I start with an idea and see where it takes me.

I like living with some spontaneity. That doesn't mean I lack structure and purpose. I know the rules of survival. However, I don't live and work like most people. The normal definitions don't apply so easily to me.

I have always struggled with my personal elevator pitch. I simply can't define myself in thirty seconds. That's even truer now that I have a new stamp in my passport of life. Survivor, near-death experience, lucky man, hemorrhagic stroke: all these terms fit, and, I could argue, none works as a definitive statement.

When everything changed for me, I placed my old life in a clear plastic box on a shelf where I could look into it every day. At first, getting back that life was my motivation to push hard and finish rehab. Now I'm not so sure I want to open that box. Oh, I'll have to crack the seal, but I think I'm only going to take out the best pieces. A redefined, newly designed Steve.

Yesterday I was talking with my friend Igor about how I am and that my art is changing.

He said, "Your road is wide open."

"It's like the salt flats," I replied.

He said, "You can go as fast as you want—no speed limits."

This was a time for me to reflect and make changes. I gave myself permission to reset and reboot. Going through a medical trauma helped me to find the strength and freedom to make changes. I thought of it as a spiritual elimination diet. I would remove everything and slowly add back what I thought I needed. If something enhanced my life, I'd keep it. The absence of detrimental influences would make room for new ideas, the freedom to experiment, and the space to grow into the person I want to be.

Life involves unpredictability. Anything can happen. Taking on its challenges should be an adventure. The difficulties should be lessons we learn from instead of adversities we simply survive. Looking at the history of my life, I can see where my footsteps have wandered.

Day 54: Wednesday, February 8, 2023

Yesterday was my follow-up visit to the neuro stroke clinic. It was two and a half hours of meeting with my team of caregivers. There were lots of questions, lots of "Move this, look here" commands. I finally looked at all the brain images. The bleed was a little bigger than a quarter. That's it. That tiny amount of blood caused so much damage. We are so fragile, and considering my recovery, incredibly resilient.

The final conclusion of the assessment is we still don't know why I had a hemorrhage. It was most likely because I had been living with slightly elevated blood pressure that spiked for some reason. I am improving beyond expectations.

"Good luck, and we'll see you in a few months for a new set of scans," I was told at the door and sent on my merry way.

I have a hard time with the lack of information as to why I had a hemorrhage in my head. I am hardwired to crave information. Without good data, how can I make informed decisions? How can I live a healthier lifestyle if I don't know what to change? I must admit, much of my anxiety is rooted in the ambiguous nature of my stroke. I met with my primary care doctor and asked him to give me guidance. After reviewing my medical records, his conclusion was not satisfying, either: "It is as if you were struck by lightning." I guess sometimes these things just happen. He reassured me that it is very unlikely to happen again.

As I've mentioned, the list of "what ifs" continues to present itself. If I stay in the moment and do not worry about the future, I find it possible to quiet the "what if?" voices in my head.

Day 55: Thursday, February 9, 2023

I wanted to wake up to a crisp-edged sunrise, one that would motivate me to get out the door early. I hoped I'd be able to strut out for a solid meditative walk and maybe to grab a few photos.

Instead, I woke up to a cold, wet morning. Gray, flat light does not get my creative mojo flowing. Instead, I buried myself under a pile of blankets and watched TV. Eventually, I decided to run errands. (I can drive all by myself. Look out world! I'm back.)

I followed my creative impulses. It's an instinct that directs me to where I should be in the moment. I found the MacArthur woods in the north Chicago metro. I sat parked in the car with the heater attempting to blow warm air on my feet and face. I looked into the dreary woods and eventually guilted myself into going for a hike.

I took off cross-country because I wanted the physical challenge. I was focusing so intently on traversing cautiously that I could not think creatively. This is a frustrating paradox of my current body limitations. I almost turned around and went back to the car. I was cold and wet and feeling disillusioned.

I pushed aside the internal conversation about my discomfort and realized there was a trail just fifty feet away. (So much for my Lewis and Clark adventures.) Moving along a safer path, less distracted, I opened up to what Mother Nature offered me. I listened with my soul, not my head. I looked without seeing what's physically in front of me and found the connection between the tactile world and my emotional experience.

I trust my intuition to guide my creativity. It is a practiced methodology that grew from years of hard work and trial and error.

I look at what is around me: the sunlight, the clouds, the shape of the landscape. I also rely on my feelings. My creative expressions are shaped by my emotional disposition. Throughout my recovery, I struggled to know my creative voice. I noted its absence due to the overwhelming nature of my stroke. I could not photograph and used my writing as my creative outlet. This changed the nature of my voice. Sharing my feelings through images is very different from writing them. As I leaned into my writing, I learned to shape the way I expressed myself with words. Through this process, I began to understand my stroke as a tool of growth and not repression.

Day 56: Friday, February 10, 2023

Today is a sweet-and-sour-shrimp day: not enough of one thing and not enough of another. I'm going to leave you to figure out that metaphor. It's not a good one, which will clue you in to my complex emotional fruit basket this morning.

This is my last day of living in the safety of my recovery nest. Tomorrow, I fly back to Florida. (I'll let you insert the bad dad joke about flapping my arms. "Hmm, it's a good thing I did a lot of upper body rehab." I couldn't resist. Sorry.)

I'm excited. I'm scared. I'm sad. I'm thrilled. I'm trying to be open and to accept this transition. Historically, I'd pluck my stakes and move my tent deeper into my emotional forest and not let anyone in. I thought I had to isolate myself to be safe and happy. I realized I don't have to be alone to be happy. I needed to build really good friendships, and I have.

A handful of the best of the best are waiting for me, friends who will be with me when I plop back in Florida. I will be living independently, but I won't be alone.

I felt like I was running from one reality to another. The weeks when I was recovering in Chicago were like a different universe. My whole stay there was one of intense purpose, and it focused entirely on my healing. It was a new thread interwoven into the larger story of my life, but it involved far greater repercussions than other threads in my tapestry. Those weeks were bending my story in a direction I had never anticipated. I feared losing the progress I had made physically and emotionally. In the next section, my writing reflects those struggles.

— FLORIDA —

I cannot say whether I was premature in pushing myself to get back to shows. Getting back to Florida by late February was my goal. But after my weekends at shows, I was in bed for two and a half days. I felt physically ill, not just tired. This began to drag me into a mild depression. I felt empty and had no energy, and this made me sad. This cycle of highs and lows lasted months. I was pushing myself to function at the level of the guy I was before my stroke. I did not grasp the futility of that expectation. This mindset kept me in an unhealthy cycle. I was having more low days than good ones. After a few days of rest, I had better energy. I'd try to be "normal," and this would send me back to bed, which led to feelings of failure. I ate poorly because I didn't have the energy to cook. I needed quality calories, not unhealthy food I thought would fill my emotional void.

I didn't share my feelings with anyone because I didn't want to look weak or be pitied. Even with all the amazing self-awareness I had achieved over the past few months, I was fighting the temptation to isolate myself. The next few months took on a different kind of recovery. My physical improvements were tangible. Battling through the emotional repercussions of my stroke took much longer. Those injuries are unseen and require patience and introspection. I didn't know it yet, but the second part of my recovery journey was just beginning.

My attempts to make it work on my terms failed. There was a point in my recovery journey, a mid-transformation state, when I was improving, but it was not far enough along to allow for my envisioned outcome.

Day 57: Saturday, February 11, 2023

Airport day.

"Holy crap! This is overwhelming. There are so many people at the airport. Many, many interweaving paths to pay attention to. Always moving. Quick stops. Lane shifts. I need to slow down."

I stood in line and bought a sandwich and couldn't find a place to sit. I walked in circles near my gate looking for a place to perch. Someone finally moved. Within minutes, a gaggle of planes loaded, and everyone was gone.

I sat. Organized my carry on. Opened my sandwich. Prepared to open the tiny pack of mustard. (Keep in mind, these small movement tasks are still hard for me.) I pinched the pack and bit into it to tear it. I added a bit of yellow color to my attire. You know what? I didn't care. My brain blew up fifty-seven days ago.

I gave myself a break. "Everything is going to be the same but with new eyes. I can't wait!"

Desperate to get back into my old life, I was determined to get on a flight from Chicago to Florida. I was physically compromised and struggled to navigate the airport.

The flight back to Florida was my first solo interaction with large groups of people. My excitement masked how weary I was from navigating one of the busiest airports in the country. After an hour of being around so many people, I was in a haze. It was as if the lights dimmed. I chose to travel alone. It would have been better to have someone accompany me. I was placing unrealistic expectations on myself.

Day 58: Sunday, February 12, 2023

"There's no place like home. There's no place like home. There's no place like home."

I had a hard time going to sleep last night because I was so excited to see the sunrise. When I finally did "go black," I slept hard, and, well, I missed the breaking of dawn. It didn't matter. It wasn't about the sun. It was about living an old habit and seeing it through new eyes.

I truly love my morning walks through the rural Florida countryside. For three years, I've paced the same route. I know the routine. But this morning was different. In the past, I was seeking an outcome. I had expectations: find a picture or a moment of meditative insight. Today the sound of my feet on the pavement synchronized with the changing morning light. The shadows from tall weeds sketched musical notes on the country lane. As I walked this familiar road with a new unfamiliarity, I was simply in the moment. I felt no anxious energy. It was clear and peaceful. I had no agenda or outcome. I was thinking without words.

Where the night sky ends

And you can see no further,

A new day begins.

I found joy in these moments: the aromas that trigger fond memories; the warble of a family of sandhill cranes; the warm, slightly damp morning air. For the first time in nearly two months, the ground under my feet felt welcoming.

Day 59: Monday, February 13, 2023

I did not write a post for this day. I was overwhelmed physically and emotionally. And after a weekend of travel and social time, I needed rest—lots of it. At first, I compared my experience to my old self. I couldn't understand why I was extremely tired. My body and brain were exhausted, and I thought I was getting sick. I needed two days in bed to begin to feel normal. I was very discouraged. Fortunately, I had support from understanding friends. They checked on me and reminded me to take it easy.

Day 60: Tuesday, February 14, 2023

In all these weeks that I've been writing about my journey, this is the first time I hesitate to share my feelings. The first words I wrote directed attention away from what I need to say, like a magician's sleight-of-hand trick. Deflection and misdirection are my most poisonous self-defenses. I need to write these words. I don't think I can grow beyond this point if I don't.

Why am I so worried about returning to my life? As I

think about this question, I feel an irrational anxiety. What is this persistent undercurrent of negative energy pounding my consciousness?

For my adult life, I've wrestled with anxiety, the fear of being less-than and laughed at. I have worried and made contingency plans for all possible outcomes. Even with my eyes closed, I made social behavior blueprints. This behavior had become my coping mechanism.

For the past two months, I have directed all my energy toward healing. I replaced the old anxious feelings with new, tangible concerns. In that process, I had lost the routine for managing the daily stressors. As I transition back to my life, unchecked waves of anxious concerns kick at my consciousness. Coming all at once, they feel horrifically daunting.

I thought I did a good job of managing the stressors of daily life. I thought I was in a good place and had a healthy base. I wasn't and hadn't. I see now that my reality was built on a foundation of stress. Adding in the unknown about my health, well, I am awakening to the painful reality that I need to make more changes.

I've had time to reflect and shine light into the dark recesses of my mind. I've been feeling anxious because, on an unconscious level, I knew I wasn't living a healthy life. The fear of returning to that life caused stress. I have to come to terms with that aspect of my personality. I need to recognize when I am getting in my own way and causing damage to myself.

I'm glad I waited to share this post. I had to go through an intense self-evaluation. A few months ago, I was creating a healthier process of dealing with my anxiety. I needed to replace that mental software with a new upgrade. I'm trusting and listening to the quiet voice that comes from my core values.

This is the hardest aspect of my personal journey, the deep emotional changes. I must keep the promise to myself not to regress to that unhealthy state of mind.

When I read this post, I think I sound like a child struggling to understand why he can't eat cake before dinner. I did not know it at the time, but a much greater awareness was just out of reach. I needed time to grow and reflect about my post-stroke body and mind.

So much self-awareness has come to the surface over the past few months. I came to terms with my dyslexic learning style. I am hardwired differently than most people. I spent most of my life trying to fit in when, at a fundamental level, that was impossible. I needed to understand where my desire to be "normal" stems from. I developed coping skills designed to allow me to slide by, never being seen, always in the shadows. I could fit into any crowd, but I was never a part of it.

I gained confidence through the recovery journey. I overcame a truly life-threatening situation to literally stand on my own two feet. I did this. I learned to accept help from others and didn't suffer the humiliation of feeling inadequate. I was not judged for being who I am. This opened my eyes. It is possible to live as the person I have hidden from everyone. The stroke happened to me, but it also happened "for" me. I now know I can accomplish anything. I have no limitations.

Day 61: Wednesday, February 15, 2023

Good morning. Writing is getting harder because I have so many distractions as I transition back to my independent life. I'm overwhelmed. I spent about four hours resting yesterday because the day before I overdid it. One of the hardest parts about returning to my former life is managing my energy and not taking on too much. I've set too many daily goals. I need to slow down and listen to my body. I have been walking every morning and doing my exercises, but mostly I'm tremendously enjoying being among friends and getting ready to go back to work.

There are no directions included when unpacking the recovery box. I must trust my body and decipher what it is telling me. I felt guilty and a bit ashamed of my diminished self. I was falling into the trap of trying to meet the expectations of friends and colleagues. They can't know what I have gone through. They knew the pre-trauma me but have yet to become acquainted with the Steve I have become. I did not pay attention to the signals my body was sending me. I believe I slowed my recovery by not resting properly.

Day 62: Thursday, February 16, 2023

Yesterday my thoughts were like a host of hummingbirds visiting a feeder, their blurred wings never stopping, slowing only long enough to taste the nectar and then fly away. I can't say I felt out of control; it was more like I couldn't find solid mental ground where my thoughts could pause. It's hard for me to give myself permission to rest. I have so much I want to accomplish. Tick, tock goes the clock.

Today I'm trying to let go of my preconceived notions and adjust my expectations. I'm holding my thoughts on today. I feel settled. Last night, I had dreams about cuddling with a big bear instead of fighting in a zombie apocalypse, which was my nighttime activity for the past week. (Smarter people than I will need to decipher that one.)

I had a long checklist of what I had to get done before my first show. As I added more activities to my daily routine, I needed more rest. This frustrated me, and in response, I kept pushing to achieve more. The day-to-day cycle of recovery is almost impossible to anticipate.

As I struggled to find "normal" for me, I failed to make the connection between mental and physical fatigue. I now know that if I overwork physically, I suffer mentally, which then manifests physically. This cycle resulted in the need for longer and longer rest periods, which dragged my attitude into a negative disposition. As I slipped into a negative mindset, I began to reject help when offered. I had done the one thing that worried me the most: I slid back into an old behavior pattern. When I feel vulnerable, I isolate myself. I did not want to be seen as weak or needy. I was pushing everyone away. Fortunately, my closest friends ignored my bad attitude and stuck with me, helping me with the transition. I am deeply thankful for their unconditional love and care.

Day 63: Friday, February 17, 2023

Buried in storage is a box of rice-paper pages telling the story of World War II as witnessed by my great uncle. Each day, he typed one sentence. Individually, they read as random thoughts, but all together, page after page, he tells a powerful narrative that spans his tour of duty in the Pacific.

This personal and intimate view of an eighteen-year-old facing death every day touched me deeply. His self-restrained use of words became a blueprint of how I tell my story. Throughout my day, I jot down thoughts and make notes. When I'm ready to write, I read through my notes and an emotional narrative begins to emerge.

Below are some of my notes from yesterday.

Walking in the wind

Strips away all sound

But the beating of your heart.

To understand beauty, you have to live in beauty.

If you're doing the same thing every day, you're going to think the same thing every day.

Getting outside will change how you think.

Live yourself into a new way of thinking.

If I am escaping from reality through artificial stimuli, how will I create a reality that I want to live?

There are no absolutes, just situations.

Start living today as the person you want to be tomorrow.

Focus on what you want to say. When you know what you want to say, then consider your audience.

Work hard. Be kind. Don't quit.

I find jotting notes throughout the day very helpful. I can reread them and see patterns of thoughts and ideas. Over time, they form a narrative that charts my personal growth, and I can see the evolution of my ideas and attitudes.

Day 64: Saturday, February 18, 2023

Maybe the fear of painful experiences measured against the ideals of an imagined life keeps us on an emotional road that we perceive as safe. However, pain and sadness force us to ask hard questions, and venturing from the known to the unknown presents an opportunity to discover more meaningful answers.

Perhaps this is the acceptance that life is hard, and the answers aren't just a phone call away. Sometimes one must change. I'm not talking about giving in or giving up; I'm suggesting a simple adjustment of expectations when it comes to desires and outcomes. It's easy to miss profound, life-shaping experiences when focusing on the result or outcome.

When given a new beginning, don't make past mistakes.

Finding and accepting answers to difficult questions changes the basic building blocks of one's life. I was emotionally living alone deep in the metaphorical woods—a long, "safe" distance from ever being accountable. What I mean is that I feared I would be judged negatively and then reminded of my inadequacies. This fear caused me to emotionally withdraw from meaningful relationships. I thought of vulnerability as a weakness. I equated emotional safety with isolation and thought I had to be alone to be happy. No one could live up to my unrealistic standards. I thought they would let me down at some point. I had not yet embraced my role in my unhappiness. This isolating attitude was a product of the defensive voices in my head. As a child, I had been told for years that I was not good enough and that I was stupid. That had emotionally scarred me. As a result, I was afraid to let anyone close to me. "Arm's length or farther, please. And don't look too closely."

Recovery was the one thing I could not do alone. My stroke forced me to accept help. I had to let go of my need to control. I did not have the energy to fight for survival as well as keep my fabricated defensive walls in place. Fundamentally, the way I had lived my life changed. Everything I knew had altered. My defensive armament meant nothing. It did not have a place in my recovery world.

In the hospital, I was a broken and vulnerable man. I had no idea how to "manage" this situation. I had to accept the unknown and let go. I needed to entertain the possibility that bad things can lead to better things. I was not judged. I was simply cared for as a person. Caregiver compassion there gave me a different kind of insight. I was liked and accepted for being me. Everyone could see through the mask I once hid behind.

I came to understand the path out of the forest starts with me. I had to make the changes. I could not expect the world to change for me. My relationships were based on my lie. I was not showing people the true me; rather, I showed them versions of the revolving masks I hid behind. If I didn't show up honestly, how could I expect to be honestly seen? Once I realized this, I changed the way I interacted with people. Instead of running away, I set personal boundaries and stood by them. I gained a deeper and more profound sense of self. I trusted my understanding of the world. This gave me the confidence to stop trying to manage every situation and to be at peace with my life and how I choose to live it.

I saw people as I wanted them to be. I judge them from a place of fear because I considered them to be threats. As my self-awareness grew and I became confident, I understood how I was judging everyone. I realized how disrespectful I was. I was not intentionally being rude; I just never gave people the chance to be themselves. We all have our own stories and baggage. I've learned to meet people where they are, not where I want them to be. My relationships are authentic and richly fulfilling. My connections are deeper and vastly rewarding. I feel a sense of contentment I had never experienced before.

Day 65: Sunday, February 19, 2023

I can only tell one story honestly, and that's mine.

There are many different methods for approaching art. I am a heart-first, technique-second artist.

I toil constantly to master the technique and methodology of my work. I want to create, by my standards, flawless images that share my emotional experiences without any barriers. In other words, I want to make a piece of art in which you don't see the

Quiet walks give me time to set positive intentions. My morning walks are for both physical and mental health.

technique, but you feel what I'm showing you. If I do this properly, the energy of my image is held in stasis until you look at it, and then, in an instant, it's released, and you make the connection. The best intentions are lost through poor execution.

Art is a means of communicating ideas. Some pieces are literal, and others are purely emotional expressions created to move you on an unconscious level. The beauty of art is that it touches every person differently. I'll give you a piece of the story by creating an emotional framework, but I leave space for you to fill in the gaps with your own story. The ultimate expression is sharing an idea I see, but you experience it through your heart.

My fundamental approach to my photography has not changed after my stroke. I still compose using the same basic methods. I build an image with strong lines and sweeping skyscapes. My color palette has softened as I've grown older. I don't use heavy colors in my imagery. What has been transformed is the subtle messages I suggest. They speak more about the joy of life. They are visually quieter. This is a hard idea to write about, but I'll give it a try. My work suggests layers of intimacy. At a distance, you will see pleasing shapes and formal compositional design—simple and elegant. As you move closer, subtle details emerge, provoking conscious and unconscious curiosity. You find an invitation to step though a visual and emotional doorway. It's a connection with the soul that expresses itself through the complexity of layers. I rarely visually "say" this is what I want you to see. Most photographs are about what the photographer sees. I create visual experiences that are about how I felt, and I share that with you.

Day 66: Monday, February 20, 2023

The rudder is tiny compared to the boat. It's a small lever that redirects a larger object.

I'm asking hard questions about my past paradigms. I'm sifting through routines, discarding some, and applying new approaches. I'm finding equilibrium between my new perspective and my old life.

I lived a routine that supported my professional and personal life. In the hospital, everything I knew was gone except for my creative intentions. Every day, this became clearer as I told my story. This honest, truthful sharing of my narrative fundamentally changed me. The transformation gave me the awareness that I would exit the forest glowing with purpose and intention.

In the past, I had a hard time making decisions. I moved at the mercy of the wind. I didn't have a rudder to guide me. I would isolate myself until I knew I was safe. I didn't feel confident. This is an honest expression of what I consider to be my greatest failure. Now, I see it, and I can change it. I know I can. I've found my rudder. I'm going to live with one hand on the tiller, living a healthy life with integrity.

My stroke and recovery were the hardest time of my life. Yet it was a gift. I believe that every situation can produce positive results. I had time to reevaluate my personal beliefs and how they were influenced by my desire to hide. I was not living the authentic me. I took the time to consider what made me feel content and happy. I was freed from the anchor of self-denial. Because I was not honoring my personal values, how could I expect to receive respect when I was not respecting myself? I had pushed my values to the side to fit in and not make waves.

Once I let go of my repressive thoughts, I was reacquainted with my values. They guide my actions and my positive outlook: I am a compassionate person who is accountable for my actions. I have integrity and am generous. Most of all, I respect others. I am living as the man I want others to see, not as the man I think they want me to be.

Day 67: Tuesday, February 21, 2023

I have a great big, stupid grin on my face, and I feel like Tigger bouncing around on my tail.

I started my morning walk in the dark and fog. About twenty minutes into my stroll down a country road, I suddenly realized I could see the sky. I walked into a clear, open area where the black was slowly turning blue, and the sun was making its presence known. As the soft light gave shape to the silhouetted trees, I began to smile and laugh.

As I witnessed the start to an amazing day, the brilliance of my life became clear: to let go of expectations and accept the perfection of nature's imperfection. Life happens, and dreams may go unrealized. Even though I physically can't achieve some of my goals, there is a wisdom gained in aging. By sharing that insight, in some small way, I will make the world a better place.

I have been a walker my whole life. When I was in the hospital, I made a pact with myself that I would enjoy my morning walks again. The idea of taking a long walk became my unspoken rehab goal. The physical health benefits are obvious. It is the mental solitude I crave. The hour I walk is a time for me to be at peace. I don't carry the burdens of the day with me. I let my thoughts wander without structure. Most days I drop into a meditative mindset. Many of my most profound moments of personal awareness were revealed while strolling in peace down a quiet country road. I never knew how much these walks meant to me until I did not have them.

Day 68: Wednesday, February 22, 2023

It gets real, real fast.

Today I will drive to Naples, Florida, because tonight a family is hosting a meet-and-greet with me and some folks from the neighborhood. I'm super excited to share my work in a very intimate and personal way.

Friday I will set up a booth at my first art fair in almost half a year.

For the past ten days, as my body allowed, I've been prepping for the show. I'm mostly ready. I had to set aside a few of my grander aspirations, but my work is framed and ready to hang. I feel relieved to have made it this far. I'm buzzing with excitement. This will be not only my first show in almost five months but also the achievement of my rehab goal. I've made it, and I am thrilled!

Over the months of my recovery, I had many moments of personal accomplishment. Being able to work, sell my images, and most importantly, make a living were truly the first big steps into self-sufficiency. My greatest lessons have come from my most adverse challenges. I appreciate what I have even more.

Day 69: Thursday, February 23, 2023

Today I set up my booth at the fair. I have set up booths at hundreds of shows over the past decade. I know what has to be done. Nothing new. Just a show. Umm … right. This is different. I am trying to not let fear creep into my attitude. I know what to do, but can I do it? I know how long a "normal" setup will take me. I planned extra time. I contacted the show to make sure I had artist friends near me, just in case. I don't know what to expect. I am trying to ensure I have support for the whole weekend.

I am all over the place. I can't get my thoughts in order. I'm not panicking, but I am struggling.

Wow! That was a tough day. All I can say is if I didn't try, I never would have forgiven myself. Fortunately, I had a great bunch of friends helping. It was hard and invigorating. It felt great to be doing something familiar after all the weeks of changes.

Day 70: Friday, February 24, 2023

Setting up for the art fair yesterday was the clearest indication of where I stand with my recovery. Assembling my booth takes a hundred sequential steps. I've done it alone for twelve years. I know the rhythm and timing of each step. Normally, fully "building" my booth takes me about four hours (a bit longer if I'm chatting with friends). If I hadn't had help yesterday, I don't think I could have finished before the moon would have lit my way. But I learned I could do it. My new approach may take longer—much longer—but I can do it!

I can't match pre-stroke Steve, yet. I'm moving slower and don't have the endurance. But I have a better idea of what I can accomplish alone. It was great to test my current self against a well-known challenge.

I was chatting with a friend a few weeks ago about the recovery process. She also had to work through a multiyear recuperation. We discussed comparing a current version of self to a past healthy version. One strategy is to only look at yesterday. I most likely will never be what I was, but if I am better than the day before, that is progress. The idea is to focus on small improvements instead of trying to do everything at once.

Day 71: Saturday, February 25, 2023

At the end of the day, the day is done. But what comes between the start and finish is the true measure of the race. It's not the victories or failures. Those are fixed and finite events that fade away. Your effort and hard work are what stay with you. They build your character and form the foundation on which you live your life.

Sitting with friends at my hotel pool, I was filled with gratitude. As we ate pizza and drank beer, I reflected on my first day back as a reforged artist.

I love sharing my work and, by extension, myself. That's always filled me with a positive, emotionally charged energy. This is what draws me to the art fair way of life. We artists are a band of like-minded individuals, all driven to share our unique, personal ways of understanding the world.

The profound depth of the connections within the artist community forms a bond that goes far beyond working together. Many, many people stopped by my booth to give hugs and support. Let's call it a reemergence day—like a birthday but with no cake.

At the end of the day, as I tried to keep up with the conversation, I was tired, as if I had run an underwater marathon. I listened to the laughter of my friends, and I can say I was truly content. My first day back. This was the first day I felt truly at home.

Back in my element! After almost three months of fear and anxiety about my life and future, I sold my photography at an art fair.

I am often reminded that life is much more than the things we do. I have a need to prove myself. Again, this goes back to the child who was told he was never good enough. As I've made the journey of recovery, I have learned to appreciate life. In the end, my end, everything I have worried about will not matter. It will all be forgotten in a few years. I guess all I have of value are my memories. They are what make my life rich and robust. They are what fill me with joy and contentment. The quest for the hidden corners of life and sharing them gives me purpose, and that's enough for me.

Day 72:
Sunday, February 26, 2023

Holy crap! I forgot how physically demanding an art fair can be. I am sore from top to bottom. It's good pain that tells me I worked hard and accomplished something, so I don't regret it. What a great experience! That's probably the most fun I've had at work in a long, long time.

Booth visitors enjoyed my work and really liked my new images. It's kind of funny: I like my work, but it now feels outdated. I've changed so much in the past couple months. I'm excited about taking some time to photograph the world and explore my writing. I'm going to shift the way I express myself, and I am excited for that to surface.

It took months for me to see the changes I was anticipating. I had to grow into this new version of me. My emotional disposition drives my art. When I enthusiastically wrote the post above, I was still dealing with the physical requirements of taking care of my body.

Day 73: Monday, February 27, 2023

My short stride

Mimics my joyful rhythm

Blissful potential

It is a decompression day. I need rest, so I'm going to take it easy. I got up as usual and went for a slow walk with the sunrise this morning.

My walk was a short stroll around the RV park where I live in the winter. I was wearing the face of success even though I was struggling. I was physically tired. I should have put aside my ego and stayed in bed.

Day 74: Tuesday, February 28, 2023

Closure, Part One: the Search for Answers

I have not changed. The physical world feels the same under my feet. I still wear socks with holes in them (all part of my grand recycling plan). Yet I am very different. The flood waters have receded, taking with them the clutter that hid my foundation. My roots, scarred with wisdom gained through age and experience, are well established.

I am an explorer by nature. I search, hoping to find the truth of the ultimate secret. I am not unhappy, but I am not content unless I'm seeking answers. I dwell on the unanswerable questions: Who am I? Why am I here? What is the meaning of my existence? I enjoy peeking under the tent flaps of life or glancing into the dark alleyways of my soul. This never-ending quest motivates me and shapes my art.

And then, in a moment, the game board was upset. The pieces of my life were tossed between the cushions of the old couch, stuck with the wrappers of long discarded memories.

What do you do when there are no answers? When you are a seeker of the universe's truths and can't find a familiar star to light your path? When you've wrapped yourself in your personal narrative and discover that it was a cloak to camouflage your accountability?

Day 75: Wednesday, March 1, 2023

Closure, Part Two: the Path Forward

As much as having a stroke was an impediment, with the right attitude, it was remarkably liberating. I was forced to set aside routines that trapped me in unhealthy, self-indulgent behaviors. I recognized I was not living my life fully because I was hindered by my doubts and fears. I restructured my daily routines with deliberate and intentional processes for success. Instead of focusing on the extremes of the emotional spectrum, I learned to recognize that both success and failure are necessary for balance. Knowledge is gained through these experiences.

As my physical vulnerability gave way to emotional vulnerability, I had to let go of control and learn to trust. Most importantly, I had to trust myself. We do not always give ourselves the best advice because we are influenced by the past and by imagined future scenarios. These influences are not always bad. They give us guidance and remind us of our fundamental values.

I've learned the importance of healthy self-reflection. I appreciate that my experiences shape me. I take the time to evaluate what I feel and what influences my emotions. Oftentimes it is simply fear of the unknown.

Some answers cannot be found until you let go of your preconceived notions. It's hard to see through the hedgerow. Follow your personal map by staying true to your beliefs and values. These are the stars that light your path.

Nobody knows why my head hemorrhaged. It doesn't matter, because in the end, it's up to me to live my life bravely and to find meaning and purpose on my terms.

Where do I go from here? Well, that's the beauty of it. I don't have to worry because I'm right here, honoring my past, excited for the future, and living in this moment, floating in a realm of blissful potential.

From the first moments in the hospital, my goal was to be here today. And, honestly, having all of you with me made it possible. From the bottom of my heart, I wish I could thank each of you personally. I'm a better man because of you. Thank you.

— INTO THE UNKNOWN:
A LEAP OF FAITH —

I told myself lies all my life because it was easier than facing the truth. I didn't really care. I lived life with a kind of reflexive, reactionary disposition. I became accustomed to the idea of an incomplete life, hitting a few highs and climbing out of the lows. I was intentionally stumbling along, safely meandering my way to nowhere. I gave lip service instead of seeking self-awareness. I was convinced I'd find the reward of happiness at some abstract point in the future. I wasn't unhappy, but I wasn't close to being at peace either.

I read books illuminating the enlightened self. I meditated and chose a positive, joyful outlook. I made a conscious effort to speak and act with a positive disposition. I did all this "work," and I was still not content. I could feel the darkness of my misalignment festering in my soul. I had only pushed it to the side. I was not ready to look at or embrace the true issue.

The problem with me or maybe the good thing about me, depending how far away you are when you look at it, is I am never content. I'm a seeker. The open road holds my attention. I'm always looking for answers. I poke my inquisitive mind into all kinds of curious places. At some point, when I open enough doors, self-illuminating discoveries are found.

Maybe simply living through enough changes of the seasons allowed me to find a form of self-awareness.

It is my disposition to look for solutions. Why was I unhappy? On the surface, my life was great, but I felt empty. I focused my attention on my inner voice. That voice is a product of life experiences. We all have one. It is the sound of our instinctive selves trying to keep us safe. It is always on patrol, looking for threats. That inner monologue is full of profound misdirected guidance. It's thousands of unconscious data points triggered by what we consciously experience. There is a mountain of wisdom in that voice, but it requires effort to interpret.

A few months before my hemorrhagic stroke, I had an epiphany. I was thinking about how my internal voice leaned heavily into the realm of unreal fantasies. I would time travel in my thoughts. I would create an alternative reality that ran parallel to my life, a place to escape to instead of looking at my self-doubts and deeply hidden fears. I would daydream about having done miraculous things and no one would judge me. A life of happiness.

Why was that voice always pushing me into the fantasy realm? I listened without acting on it. I began to understand. It was trying to protect me from being hurt. That led down a new path, one that forced me to explore why I was feeling pain.

I finally figured it out. I grew up in a time when people with learning disabilities or different learning styles were mostly rejected by the system. I was never encouraged. I was never given opportunities to excel. I grew up thinking I was stupid. I could never match my abilities with the expectations. I coped with the inadequate feelings by slipping away into safe havens in the corners of my mind. I had programmed myself to push people away and hide because I didn't want to be hurt.

After my brain bleed, I learned to use that voice as a means of pushing forward. I flipped it around. Now when I hear that voice in my head, I stop and reflect. I inspect it from a dispassionate perspective. I recognize its tone and understand that I have a challenge in front of me. Instead of making excuses or assuming that I'm not good enough, I dig in and face the challenge.

I have stepped into the unknown, gratefully embracing that I have discovered something fundamental about myself, and I have begun to wake up and feel a greater type of confidence growing, not one of defense or fear but one that simply embraces and nurtures my gift. It fosters the transformation I am undergoing.

— TRANSFORMATION —

The imprecise moment arrives with the soft fluttering of gradual self-awareness. You realize you are changing. I don't mean physically; that's obvious and instantaneous. It's the internal self. Your understanding of life is different because you have experienced and survived something very rare.

It's not a profound revelation screaming at you from the darkness or thumping you on the head and transforming your life. It's more like taking your first slow, deep breath. It fills your soul with a sense of peace and calm, and you intuitively know you are different, changed.

I feel that all the complex aspects of my diverse personality are finally synchronized. It is a profound, conscious understanding within an unconscious process. I realize I have let go of my past self and the expectations that came with that Steve.

There was a point when I knew I could do nothing other than let go. When my body broke, I was physically transformed. I relearned instinctive movements. My brain became reacquainted with fundamental survival skills. I relearned the movements I mastered as a toddler and appreciated how much harder it was with an adult's intellect. This kind of reorientation opens a different self-understanding, a pathway to revisiting my long-buried core values.

The artist is an explorer of the impossibly furtive realm of the self. I am driven by the possibility of finding new connections between seemingly unrelated points of information. I combine my emotions, ideas, and experiences into a distinctly unique voice. To create in this nebulous space requires time, discipline, and most of all, full concentration.

As my physical world transformed, I found refuge living in the moment. Instead of worrying about what I lost or comparing myself to the past, I met myself where I was. I accepted this new version of me. That became my bridge into a steadier understanding of myself. And in turn, it gave me a solid connection with my creative space.

By accepting both the repercussions of my hemorrhagic stroke and the process of recovery, I began a profound and life-changing transformative process.

— AWARENESS —

I thought I'd discovered deep awareness. What I was living was a watered-down version. It wasn't until I went through the physical and mental changes from my stroke that I truly began to understand. Traumatic experiences transform us and open the doorway to untapped awareness.

Our lives are pre-programmed for the customs of daily life. We are indoctrinated into a system of social survival. We count on the predictability of daily life to give us purpose and meaning. When we go through a rapid transformative experience, everything is stripped away. We are left clinging to the few tangible aspects of life. Finding purpose and meaning is almost impossible because that ideal is bound to our rituals and lifestyles.

After a life altering event, we physically change, and we look for answers. It's natural to turn inward and listen to those voices that whisper desperate thoughts. They are speaking from old memories and experiences. I stopped comparing the current Steve with the Steve shrouded in memory. I let go of that physical self. This decluttered the path to accepting my new self. With fewer distractions, I freed up headspace and opened myself to discovering a new self-awareness.

I stopped looking for answers to why, and instead looked for answers to how I might live my life. How will I move forward? I intentionally saw my life with relevance, purpose, and meaning. A new normal.

As I turned inward, I listened to the thoughts that brought me anxiety and discomfort and to those that brought me peace and calm. I looked closely at their underlying motivations. I replaced what I was with what I will be. I chose to move forward with my life, no matter what my physical condition. It is the alignment of my beliefs, my desires, and my general positive disposition.

The only way out is to look at the broader picture. When confronted with a triggering event, listen to that negative voice, and determine its root cause. See it in the greater context of life, not just in one frame.

Awareness isn't a magical destination. It takes focused dedication and the intention of change. It is a sixth sense that draws on a combination of the other five, a sensory experience. You will know you're doing the right thing because anxiety will be absent. Without the distractions of a "normal" daily life, you will feel aligned and synchronized. When it feels right, move yourself in that direction. Over time, you will learn to trust yourself and find the strength to thrive.

— REDEMPTION —

I've written pages about self-forgiveness. It's a very personal experience. I needed to go through this process. Forgiving myself is the decision to accept who I am today. I didn't discover a magic pill to solve all my problems. It's taken a lot of work—hours and hours of self-reflection. Going through a traumatic life change forced me to reevaluate my relationship with myself. Here, I will share what I have written on that topic. Maybe you will find some wisdom or some value.

Before I could forgive myself, I had to dismantle my emotional barriers. Often, I'd sense a metaphorical wall I could not see over. I became comfortable with never looking past it. I was growing content with the predictable and known. I found excuses to justify the voices that secretly reminded me not to raise my head. "Keep your feet on the safe trail."

Existing in that space becomes a piece of who you are. Living intensely with one emotional thread creates a psychological drug that sustains an unhealthy narrative. Dysfunctional spaces feel normal when revisited repeatedly. Even though it may not be healthy, it feels familiar and comfortable.

I shuffled along in unconscious frustration. My memories

flashed through my mind like frames from old home movies, giving me glimpses of a blurry, faded, black-and-white childhood. They included laughter and pain, hard-learned lessons, and soft landings. It's a collection of bits and pieces, like a roadmap with many blank spaces.

I loathed my personal history, and I was held back by the fear of judgment. As I looked at my life, I saw more dark failures than bright high points.

It has taken me years to understand what was happening inside my mind. There was a duality of experiences: the external, which wanted to be outgoing and take on life's challenges, and that internal voice that held me back: "Don't let others see the real you. They will hurt you."

Once I woke up to this duality, I faced that voice of my childhood fears. I embraced that part of me and began to use it in a positive way. I watched those old movies from a distance, and I could see the whole story, not just a trailer. I used the awareness of that voice to overcome my fears. Because I knew it was there, I could ignore it or use it as a tool. I could see the red flag, and it reminded me of where I don't want to be in life. I know myself, my intentions, and my integrity. I rely on those instead of on that negative voice.

Maybe I was afraid to make changes, afraid that if I reached for true contentment and inner joy, I'd have to emerge from under the safety of my comfortable blankets. I could be exposed to the recrimination of those I feared. Maybe I'm using my stroke as an excuse to evolve. I mean, who's going to pass judgment on the victim?

To love and accept myself, I had to learn to live with my less-proud moments. I am made up from my experiences—all the ugly and the beautiful pieces, all that I fear and revere. I am composed of a lifetime of failures and accomplishments, trials and errors, and regrets and triumphs. Trying to hide the ugly bits meant I was living a lie. It meant my life was built on a false narrative and I was not taking personal responsibility.

Breaking this barrier is an incredibly personal journey. There's no medal for winning, and there's no second place. This is the portal to the meaning of life. Come through this, and live a full life.

— VULNERABILITY —

What comes to mind when I say "vulnerable"? Is it weakness? A lack of confidence? Powerlessness and loss of personal control? Is vulnerability the absence of strength? Victimhood?

I would combat feeling vulnerable with being prepared. I created a response for every contingency. Every time my unconscious voice spoke, I would listen and prep for the worst. I was an obsessive, strategic planner. My mind would free-fall into a defensive mode that told me, "They are going to hurt me," or "I'll look stupid, so I better be prepared." I think I wasted a third of my life dreaming up contingency plans for fantasized or perceived threats.

Never in all my defensive musings was there a plan for a stroke. I had lost all control. I had to turn inward before I could look outward. My stroke dramatically changed my life in a matter of minutes. I was lost and afraid. In the absence of normal daily routines, I found myself. I took solace in my personal mantra. I looked past the role I was playing, and I began to accept and appreciate myself for my strengths and weaknesses.

What does vulnerability mean to me now? It's giving up control and discovering trust. Trusting my judgments. Loving and honoring myself. Knowing who I am gives me the foundation to trust without expectation. It is humbling to be physically vulnerable. It is gracious to be emotionally vulnerable. By letting down my walls, I invited people into my life. I am less judgmental and more comfortable meeting people where they are. Emotional and social vulnerability takes bravery. This courage will carry into every aspect of my life. People will accept me for who I am—not for the masks I wear but for my authenticity. From being physically vulnerable, I learned about what it means to be safe with emotional vulnerability.

— GOALS —

When I get lost in the doldrums of my personal trauma, I find respite in pointing my mental energy toward distant goals. I keep my intentions on the overall outcome, but I pay careful attention to each step. Each small step brings me closer to my goal. This is how I choose the nature and quality of my future. Life happens, but I can plan the kind of life I want to live.

I anticipate missteps along the way, but creative problem-solving can arise through them. I think of mistakes as life's editing process. Once I've tried something and it doesn't work, I don't think about it anymore. I remove it from my mental checklist. If I fixate on what hasn't worked, I will not have room in my mind to find a different path toward my goal. I rethink the problem in context of my overall goal and come up with a different way to achieve my next step. This keeps me moving without feeling the weight of failure.

Let's say I want to sell a million digital copies of this book. Do I cross my fingers and passively hope for a miracle? I look at my grand goal. I don't fixate on the massive gap between here and there. I take small, achievable steps directed toward my overall objective. I might email ten people and ask them to each email ten people about my book. Ultimately, I choose how to manage my future life by taking the appropriate steps today.

Do the work and don't be afraid to make mistakes. That's how we learn. If we had all the answers, life would be boring.

My success is rooted in the footsteps I take on my recovery journey.

— DEPARTURES —

I've arrived at a vast emotional plain. It's not a crossroads but a gradual rise that offers a moment of choice. The bounty of opportunities reaches toward the horizon, but when I look down, the path might be obscured in a haze of indecision. The endless number of possibilities can freeze me. My past could secure my feet in deep ruts. When I pull back and look at my life in a larger context, I can gain awareness that this is not a new quandary. Throughout my life, I've repeatedly asked myself, "What's the next step?"

I am no longer content to drift and allow life to happen to me. My path has been defined by reacting to the conditions tossed onto my track. Hardships are inevitable, but how I respond is in my control. It's the choice we all face: the universe happens to us, and we choose how to adapt.

I made a contract with myself. I have set internal boundaries. When I face obstacles, I have a personal framework to navigate them. I will continue to react to and to live with the randomness of the universe. But now I will do it with a sense of purpose, intention, and most importantly, integrity.

Every morning, the same sun rises, but each sunrise gives us light to see a new day.

— A WILDFLOWER IN A FIELD OF WILDFLOWERS —

I had a panic attack recently. I could not get out of my head. Fearful thoughts flashed into my mind faster and darker than I could fight them off. "What if?" floated to the surface. I felt the oppressive weight of incomprehension and indecision. My thoughts ran together, overwhelming my capacity to rationally organize my defenses. I was desperate. I called friends who graciously gave me the time and space to find my way forward. I cried and babbled my thoughts as they stacked up. I vented and eventually exorcised those demons. As my mind settled, I found my mental discipline. I stepped back from the irrational, fear-based thoughts and looked at them from a healthy perspective.

Trauma is a horrible twist of fate. In an instant, your life is changed. The feeling of loss is, at times, a seemingly impossible weight to carry. Without the help of an amazing support network, I could not have survived. Trauma is not something to live through alone. Find help. It is there. Learning to receive and accept advice and guidance saved me.

Recovering from a traumatic event is a lifelong process, but with a positive, healthy attitude and a supportive network of friends and professionals, it is possible to grow and find a greater sense of peace and wellbeing. My journey has only begun. I've chosen to get on with living my life. I still have my dark days. I try to see each one as a piece of my emotional landscape, one flower in a field of wildflowers.

I wish I could tell you that I am one hundred percent healed and whole, that fear and questions and doubts are no longer my companions. But I still have days when I'm weary. I have moments when the overwhelming weight of everyday life sits heavily in my soul. However, I've created life-affirming strategies to find my way out of these dark spaces.

I am genuinely excited to live my life. I've been given a new chance to reevaluate and make fundamental changes. I don't feel the unconscious worry and anxiety that ruled my life before my stroke. I've given myself permission to live the life I want to live. I seek joy and contentment in the little moments. I've embraced the idea of releasing the past and not worrying about the future, of simply living in the here and now, in this moment. I have a plan for how I want to live my life. In other words, I have a plan shaped around what I want my life to feel like.

I'm not trying to give you the answers but to simply point you in a positive, healthy direction. It is up to you to take the first steps. It is possible to live a better life.

– ABOUT THE AUTHOR –

Steve Wewerka is a writer and photographer whose works have appeared in such publications as *Life Magazine, Time Magazine, Sports Illustrated, The New York Times,* and many others over his forty-year career. His work focuses on the intimate explorations of the human condition.

He lives in Florida and Wisconsin when he's not traveling throughout the country, blogging about his experiences and photographing the beauty he encounters. You can read more of his writing and view his photographs at https://stevewewerka.com/ and on YouTube and Instagram.